MACKEREL AND THE MAKING OF
BALTIMORE, COUNTY CORK
1879–1913

Maynooth Studies in Local History

GENERAL EDITOR   Raymond Gillespie

This pamphlet is one of eight new additions to the Maynooth Studies in Local History series in 1999. Like their twenty predecessors, most are based on theses submitted for the M.A. in Local History at National University of Ireland, Maynooth. The pamphlets are not concerned primarily with the portrayal of the history of 'particular places'. All are local in their focus but that localisation is determined not by administrative boundaries but rather the limits of the experience of everyday life in the regions of Ireland over time. In some of these works the local experience is of a single individual while in others social, occupational or religious groups form the primary focus of enquiry.

The results of these enquiries into the shaping of local societies in the past emphasises, again, the diversity of the Irish historical experience. Ranging across problems of economic disaster, political transformation, rural unrest and religious tension, these works show how such problems were grounded in the realities of everyday life in local communities. The responses to such challenges varied from region to region, each place coping with problems in its own way, determined by its historical evolution and contemporary constraints.

The result of such investigations can only increase our awareness of the complexity of Ireland's historical evolution. Each work, in its own right, is also a significant contribution to our understanding of how specific Irish communities have developed in all their richness and diversity. In all, they demonstrate the vibrancy and challenging nature of local history.

Maynooth Studies in Local History: Number 22

Mackerel and the Making of Baltimore, County Cork 1879–1913

Séamus Fitzgerald

IRISH ACADEMIC PRESS

DUBLIN • PORTLAND, OR

First published in 1999 by
IRISH ACADEMIC PRESS
44, Northumberland Road, Dublin 4, Ireland
and in the United States of America by
IRISH ACADEMIC PRESS
c/o ISBS, 5804 NE Hassalo Street, Portland, OR 97213.

website:www.iap.ie

British Library Cataloguing in Publication Data
Fitzgerald, Seamus
    Mackerel and the making of Baltimore, County Cork, 1879–1913. – (Maynooth studies in local history; 22)
    1. Mackerel fisheries – Ireland – Baltimore – History   2. Baltimore (Ireland) – Economic conditions
    I. Title
    338.3 727782

    ISBN 0716526816

Library of Congress Cataloging-in-Publication Data
Fitzgerald, Séamus.
    Mackerel and the making of Baltimore, County Cork, 1879–1913/Séamus Fitzgerald.
        p.   cm. — (Maynooth studies in local history no. 22)
    Includes bibliographical references and index.
    ISBN 0–7165–2681–6 (pbk.)
    1. Baltimore (Ireland) — History. 2. Mackerel fisheries—Ireland—Baltimore—History. 3. Mackerel fisheries—Ireland—Cork (County)—History. I. Title.
    II. Series.
    DA995.B19F58   1999
    941.9 5—dc21   99–27212
                                                                    CIP

Typeset in 10 pt on 12 pt Bembo by
Carrigboy Typesetting Services, County Cork
Printed by ColourBooks Ltd, Dublin

Contents

Acknowledgements

My preoccupation with past communities centred around Baltimore introduced me to a living community to whose members I am indebted in varying degrees, not only for facilitating access to those elusive sources, but also for their professional expertise, personal encouragement and friendship.

Dr. Raymond Gillespie, as Course Director, combined both mastery of his subject with generous personal support and advice. My supervisor, Dr. Carla King, was a constant source of encouragement and guidance in monitoring my progress and clarifying my direction. Dr. Mary Ann Lyons, while acting as Course Director, freely gave of her time and expertise. I am also grateful to the members of my class and especially, Seán O Sullivan and Liam Clare for their friendship and co-operation. I acknowledge the inspirational role of the maritime scholarship of Dr. John de Courcy Ireland, Maritime Institute of Ireland.

In the search for sources I have been fortunate to have had the assistance of many people. These include in particular, Philip O'Regan, Skibbereen; Tim Cadogan, archivist Cork Co. Library; Donal Lynch, Traditional Boats of Ireland; Éamonn Lankford, Iarsmalann Chléire; in Baltimore, Rev. T. O'Donovan, Bernie and Bernard O'Driscoll, Richard Bushe, Patrick O'Driscoll, Roger Hislop, Alfred O'Mahony; Dolly O'Reilly, Sherkin Island. I am grateful also to the staffs of various archives including: Maynooth College; Brian Donnelly, Rena Lohan, Caitríona Crowe, National Archives; Jim O'Shea, John O'Sullivan, National Library; Dr. Dáithí Ó hÓgáin, Criostóir Mac Cárthaigh, Bairbre Ní Fhloinn, Roinn Béaloideas Éireann; Dr. Liam Hyde and Mary Doyle, Department of Agriculture; David Griffith and John Molloy, Marine Institute; Nicky O'Malley, Land Commission; Mark Farrell, Department of Education; Gerard Whelan, Royal Dublin Society; *Southern Star*, Skibbereen; My colleagues in Dundrum College, especially Brian Dornan as mentor, Seán Conroy, Paddy Glynn, Marty Fallon, David Byrne have given me the benefit of their time and expertise as have Catherine and Mick O'Meara, Dominic Dillane, Antoinette Dornan, Angela and Steve Gaffey.

I am very grateful to Noel Casey for his unfailing and generous help with his computer expertise and incisive comments. My brothers, Eamonn and Mícheál have assisted me in various ways at crucial stages. I owe a special debt to Jill Schofield for her depth of understanding and loving support. This study is dedicated to my parents, Mary and the late Moss Fitzgerald, my first teachers and primary sources.

Introduction

Daniel Donovan's *Sketches in Carbery* published in 1876 contrasted the sixteenth-century prosperity of Baltimore town in County Cork with 'its quiet unpretending and un-business like appearance' three centuries later.[1] In 1887, however, Baltimore was described 'as having been transformed by it [the fishing industry] from one of the most miserable of Irish villages into a prosperous and thriving neighbourhood'.[2] This study seeks to investigate this transformation in terms of its maritime economy and society. The turning of the tide for Baltimore and its environs, may be said to have begun with the appointment in 1879 of Fr Charles Davis as parish priest of Baltimore, and the financial support of English philanthropist Baroness Burdett-Coutts for the fishermen of Cape Clear. The collaboration of these two individuals coincided with the locational advantages which Baltimore enjoyed. This study concentrates on the mackerel industry as the other fisheries such as herring, salmon or lobster did not have the same significance for Baltimore between 1879 and 1913.

The revival of the fishing industry in Baltimore towards the end of the nineteenth century and the prosperity it brought to Baltimore and the surrounding district were seen by contemporary critics of Ireland's failure to exploit its fishing resources as a model for Ireland as a whole. This revival coincided with the Land Question which dominated the public consciousness at local and national levels. Likewise scholarly attention has largely been focused on the land-based aspects of the rural economy to the neglect of the maritime dimension. This is reinforced by the difficulty of accessing a central strong source, comparable to the maritime equivalent of landed estate records. Maritime records for the period tend to be disparate and sometimes incomplete due to the fluctuating fortunes of sea based activities and the variety of maritime organisations both governmental and commercial. Ironically, despite dissatisfaction with the efforts of various government bodies responsible for developing the maritime economy during our period, the surviving records of organisations such as the Board of Works, the Board of Trade, the Congested Districts Board, the Department of Agriculture and Technical Instruction and even Crime Branch Special files are the major primary sources. No less important are the parliamentary papers which are a rich source for maritime information and statistics relating to Baltimore and its environs. Newspapers such as the *West Cork Eagle*, popularly known as the *Eagle* and located in Skibbereen, regular reports of the operations of the mackerel industry with Fr Davis receiving prominent coverage. Fr Davis, himself, in his pamphlet, *Deep*

Sea Fisheries of Ireland,[3] portrays Baltimore's 'astonishing progress' as a fishing port in the context of a historical review of the fluctuating fortunes of the Irish fishing industry, along with imaginative but practical remedies for its improvement. The special reports presented to the Royal Dublin Society and the Congested Districts Board by Rev. W.S. Green, a contemporary of Fr Davis, combine contemporary scientific knowledge with a valuable personal insight into the functioning of the Baltimore mackerel industry in relation to Ireland, England and the United States of America.

A complementary and local perspective is evident in the folklore relating to the Baltimore area in the Department of Irish Folklore, University College Dublin. Of particular significance is the material collected from fishermen. Conchúr Ó Síocháin's autobiography, *Seanchas Chléire,*[4] and also the folklore of fisherman Seán Ó hAo in *Seanachas ó Chairbre 1*[5] provides us with some of the few accounts of the life of a mackerel fisherman. Otherwise, personal or administrative records emanating from Baltimore district itself vary from lost, as in the case of Baltimore and Skibbereen Harbour Board, or unavailable for legal reasons, as in the case of the Baltimore Fishery School.

Cormac Ó Gráda has already acknowledged the singular contributions of contemporary maritime historians, John de Courcy Ireland and Vivienne Pollock, when 'curiously, the history of the Irish fishing industry has been little studied'.[6] John de Courcy Ireland's *Ireland's Sea Fisheries: a History*, apart from providing a national overview of the fishing industry over time, sufficiently highlighted Baltimore's largely forgotten contribution to recent maritime history to encourage this study to explore it in greater depth between 1879 and 1913.

The first section describes Baltimore's maritime location and resources. The economic impact of the mackerel industry on Baltimore and its environs are examined in the second part. While attempting to define the reasons why Baltimore became a centre of the mackerel industry, which had previously been dominated by Kinsale, it also explores the factors which caused it to be dominated by outsiders and unable to sustain its leading position as a distribution centre for mackerel. The infrastructural changes which the mackerel industry stimulated in Baltimore and the agents of change are the chief focus of the third section. Consequently, the natural advantages which Baltimore enjoyed as a landing place for the international mackerel fleet in 1879 are juxtaposed with the inadequacy of the man-made facilities for the processing, distribution and exporting of the mackerel. Finally, the process of social and political change which the community in Baltimore experienced in the context of the mackerel industry is examined. The seasonal and international character of this industry encouraged a network of interacting communities rather than a static or homogenous society.

Baltimore and the Sea

Baltimore is a small town in West Cork. The townland of Baltimore in which it is located is surrounded by the sea except along its eastern boundary. The town overlooks a 'fine natural harbour'[1] protected by a chain of islands. To the north are Spanish Island and Ringarogy Island, while its western boundary is shielded from the Atlantic Ocean by Sherkin Island. Offering further shelter is an outer ring of islands, the largest and most southerly of which is Cape Clear, a distance of eight miles from Baltimore. Though the harbour may be entered by the North Channel through the islands, the southern entrance leads directly from the Atlantic between Sherkin island and the southern extremity of Baltimore townland.

Baltimore's natural advantages as a harbour of refuge were enhanced in the days of sail by its proximity to Cape Clear Island, Fastnet Rock and Mizen Head which were frequently used as landmarks for vessels seeking to make a landfall in southern Ireland.[2] In the terse language of the Admiralty, 'it offered . . . the only chance of safety . . . to a vessel embayed between Stag rocks and Cape Clear'.[3] Baltimore's nautical nodality also extended inland to Skibbereen, the largest town in West Carbery. The river Ilen, which flows into Baltimore harbour, provides access to Skibbereen ten miles upstream. In 1883 vessels of up to 196 tons were able to navigate upstream as far as Old Court where cargo could be transhipped in lighters to or from Skibbereen, a further distance of two and a half miles.[4]

Regarded as the most ancient town in West Carbery,[5] certainly in the eighteenth century Baltimore was not a prosperous town. The failure of the people of Baltimore to capitalise on the fish in their local waters is confirmed by Richard Pococke' portrayal of it in 1758 as a place of 'only a few cabins' with the 'old Castle' reduced to a state of ruin.[6] In 1833 Lord Carbery[7] shared the cost of building what Samuel Lewis in 1837 regarded as 'a substantial pier', although he describes it being 'small' a few sentences later.[8] Lewis highlighted the value of the pier as a landing place for Cape Clear fishermen who at this time 'were wholly employed in fishing' and had established a market for cured fish.[9] While Lewis praised the Cape Clear men for being 'expert and resolute seamen',[10] he made no reference to Baltimore based fishermen. His belief that Baltimore 'though small, is rapidly increasing in size and importance' was based on the observation that 'several large and handsome houses have been recently built and others are in progress'.[11] This contrasts with the 1835 inquiry into the municipal corporations of Ireland which concluded that in Baltimore 'there is no manufacture, and the town is very poor and does not seem to be improving'.[12] Both the Commission of Inquiry of 1835 and Lewis concurred

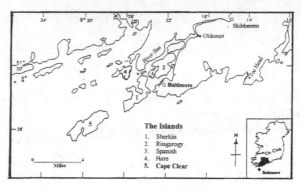

1. Baltimore and the Islands

that the port of Baltimore attracted a variety of shipping traffic.[13] However, 'the considerable coasting trade, consisting principally of the export of corn and potatoes' mostly related to 'Skibbereen and other places higher up the channel than the town of Baltimore'.[14]

Overall, the people of Cape Clear island suffered more than the people of Baltimore during and after the Famine. The post-Famine destitution of the islanders was aggravated by exceptional distress in 1862 which prompted the Catholic parish priest, Fr Leader, to appeal for help to a Miss[15] Angela Burdett-Coutts, a wealthy but philanthropic English woman.[16] Her generous response to a report of 31 October 1862, commissioned by herself, spearheaded a series of innovative projects which benefited the communities of both Cape Clear and Baltimore, especially from 1879 onwards.[17] She believed that, in the long term, the prosperity of the islanders lay in the revival and development of the fishing industry. Traditionally, fishing in Cape Clear was primarily focused on feeding the family rather than supplying a market economy.[18] Despite notable exceptions, as in the case of the Kinsale and Arklow fisheries, the subsistence economy of the Cape Clear fishermen typified the low level of enterprise among Irish fishermen in the 1860s.[19] This contrasted with 'the Cornish, Manx and Scotch, men who came hundreds of miles 'to our shores to reap the ocean harvest.'[20]

A solution to 'The Irish Fishery Question', as it was termed in 1876,[21] was initiated at a local level in 1879 by Baroness Burdett-Coutts with the co-operation of the Cape Clear fishermen. The success of this initiative became synonymous with the transformation of Baltimore from 'a decaying village' to the 'centre of a great industry'.[22] The baroness recognised that, if the Cape Clear fishermen were to emulate the success of their foreign counterparts, they needed the capital to invest in the bigger and better equipped boats suitable for deep-sea fishing rather than the traditional 'crazy open hooker'.[23] The baroness provided half the cost of the boat as an interest free loan which was repayable annually over a period as long as twenty years.[24] The repayments were to be paid into a permanent £10,000 fund established by the baroness in 1880 so that the money could be used for further loans.[25] In one year from

1880 to 1881 the Cape Clear fleet increased from eight to fifteen vessels, largely financed by £5,000 from the fund.[26]

It is no accident that the initiation of the Burdett-Coutts fund and its subsequent successful implementation both by the fishermen of Cape Clear and the Baltimore district coincided with the appointment of Rev. Charles Davis as parish priest of Baltimore and the islands in 1879.[27] Having already lived among the people of both Cape Clear and Sherkin as a young curate and having witnessed their poverty, despite being close to rich fishing grounds, he became convinced that, if fishing were fostered as an industry, it would bring prosperity to all coastal communities.[28] Furthermore, his stated belief in 1880 that 'the want of capital, appliances, and proper gear to catch the fish'[29] was the key to the problem of poverty concurred with the aims of the Baroness Burdett-Coutts fund. In his own words he willingly became 'the instrument through which have passed the munificent grants of a noble lady'.[30]

The fruitful collaboration between an English philanthropic lady and an Irish Catholic priest was based on a similar approach to the value of developing the fishing industry. Correspondence between them reveals a shared belief that the provision of capital alone would not ensure that either the islanders or the people of mainland Baltimore would be able to pursue sea-fishing beyond subsistence level (regarded as eking out a 'miserable existence' by Fr Davis).[31] Both the baroness and Fr Davis agreed on the necessity of combining capital with a system of education that would inculcate an entrepreneurial mentality based on thrift and self-reliance.[32] A practical expression of this philosophy was the opening of the Baltimore Industrial School on 17 August 1887 by Baroness Burdett-Coutts with Fr Davis as one of its trustees and first manager.[33] It was Baltimore's good fortune that the appointment of Fr Davis as parish priest in 1879 would provide the leadership that would enable it to recover some of its former prosperity based on its maritime resources.

2. Baroness Angela Burdett-Coutts (1814–1906) (courtesy Coutts Archive London)

3. Fr Charles Davis (1827–1892) (courtesy Cape Clear Museum Collection)

The Economic Impact of the Baltimore Mackerel Industry

The Baltimore of 1879, to which Fr Davis had been appointed as parish priest, was described on the occasion of his premature death in 1893 as 'a miserable town, which had drifted to decay apparently beyond hope of resurrection'.[1] The historical accuracy of this description may be a little tainted by journalistic hyperbole. There were tentative signs of a fishing revival as exemplified by the founding of the Baltimore Fishery Company, in 1878.[2] The writer's pessimism may also have been intensified by the association of 1879 with the appalling distress, bordering on famine proportions, experienced in particular by the coastal communities of the south and west of Ireland.[3] A succession of bad harvests since 1877 had had a disastrous effect on the potato crop, still the staple food of many people.[4] Only half the crop had been saved in the Skibbereen Union by October 1879 but Mr. W. A. Power, the Local Government inspector, was of the opinion that the people of Cape Clear and those along the coast would derive some advantage from fishing which they had not done during the 1840s famine.[5] As the agricultural crisis deteriorated over the winter of 1879 and into the spring of 1880, the long term value of developing a complimentary maritime economy was given some recognition by relief measures for the benefit of fisheries consisting of a donation of £20,000 from the Canadian parliament and a sum of £45,000 from the English parliament.[6] Baltimore itself benefited by a grant of £200 from the Canadian Fund and £3,000 from the English parliament for a new fishery pier whose construction commenced in 1880.[7] The success of Baroness Burdett-Coutts's financial support for the fishermen of Cape Clear, initiated in 1879 with the aid of Fr Davis, was used as an argument for funding the purchase of fishing boats from relief funds.[8]

The importance of the mackerel fishery to Baltimore is revealed in a *Cork Examiner* report of the visit of the lord mayor of Dublin to the town on 22 April 1880, in connection with the Mansion House Relief Fund, when it stated that 'things are beginning to look bright now on account of the mackerel fishing season having commenced. No complaints were made of destitution here'.[9] Equally optimistic was Commander Tuckling of *H.M.S. Goshawk* who, while delivering a quantity of meal and clothes to Fr Davis at Baltimore July 1880, concluded that the distress was at an end in the district.[10] While singling out the aptitude of the area fishermen from the Baltimore for mackerel fishing and recommending support in the form of nets, he obviously felt that local involvement in the mackerel fishery was still in its infancy.[11] Thus he suggested that 'these men' should learn from the outsiders by catching 'the spirit of emulation and so take to this fishery more than they otherwise would ...'[12]

'This fishery', up to and including 1880, had been termed the 'Kinsale Mackerel Fishery', as it had been initiated in Kinsale in 1862 by a Mr. Robert Cronin of the Isle of Man, using Manx fishing luggers.[13] The fishing was conducted on a seasonal basis of twelve weeks after the spring mackerel arrived to spawn off the coast, usually after mid-March. It was primarily an export trade to the principal cities of England, such as London, Birmingham, Manchester and Liverpool. The fresh mackerel, packed in ice at Kinsale, from 1869 onwards was transported in steamers principally to the port of Milford Haven for distribution by rail.[14] The main elements of this successful trade, namely, catching, buying and transporting, were dominated by English, Manx and Scotch people whose fishing fleet in 1876 consisted of a combined fleet of 230 vessels in contrast with 133 Irish vessels.[15] By 1879, even though the number of United Kingdom vessels increased by 44 per cent to 308 vessels, the Irish fleet had increased by 39 per cent to 218 vessels.[16]

Paradoxically, the havoc wrought by nature on the agrarian based economy between 1877 and 1880 contrasted with the unexpected bounty of the sea. This was brought about by an unexpected change in the migrating patterns of the mackerel shoals which were reported in 1879 to be concentrating closer to Baltimore.[17] Consequently, the mackerel boats, both foreign and Irish, increasingly found Baltimore and the other ports to the west more convenient than Kinsale for landing their catches. 1880 marked the turning of the tide for Baltimore when its new found status as a landing place for spring mackerel was officially acknowledged by the inspectors of Irish fisheries in the 1880 annual return of mackerel landings where it was the only port other than Kinsale for which returns were provided.[18]

Though landings of 237,436 cwts. at Kinsale dwarfed 19,690 cwts. at Baltimore, Kinsale's monopoly of the mackerel fishery was ended. The changing nature of the mackerel industry is illustrated in Figure 4 below. In 1881 four other ports were included with Kinsale and Baltimore in the official returns.[19] By 1890 the number of ports had increased to a total of eighteen in Cork and Kerry alone.[20]

Since the success of the Kinsale mackerel fishery had confirmed the demand for fresh spring mackerel in England, Baltimore's natural advantage of a good harbour adjacent to rich fishing grounds gave it a strong competitive edge. A major obstacle in 1879 to the development of its natural resources was the undeveloped nature of the man-made infrastructure which impeded the speedy landing and distribution of the mackerel whose market value depended on freshness. This was exemplified by the unsuitability of the town's only pier for an increasing mackerel fleet.

The fishery inspector Mr. Hayes claimed that, despite its inadequate landing facilities, Baltimore had 'assumed an importance as a centre for a large portion of the mackerel fleet that was simply astonishing'.[21] Certainly, 1880 represented a new beginning, if not a resurrection, for Baltimore, even if its portion of the mackerel fleet was hardly large that year. In fact the official returns reveal that 569 vessels fished from Kinsale compared with forty from Baltimore.[22] The Board of Trade granted permission for the construction of the new fishery pier on 6 December 1880.[23]

Baltimore's rising importance as a landing place for spring mackerel was confirmed in the 1881 fishery returns which reported that its mackerel landings had increased by 75.2 per cent in volume and 59.8 per cent in value. Kinsale, however, while its landings were 377.3 per cent greater in volume than those of Baltimore, experienced a decline of 30.6 per cent in volume and 33.8 per cent in value. Juxtaposed with the returns was the prediction that: 'Baltimore, in all probability, will become ultimately the head-quarters of the Southern Mackerel Fishery as, from its position, the fishing grounds can be reached from it with less delay than from other harbours'.[24]

The 1881 prediction about Baltimore's pivotal position in the mackerel fishery was based on the assumption that the spring mackerel shoals, whose mercurial migration habits had already affected Kinsale's mackerel fishery, would consistently return to Baltimore every fishing season from March until June but predictability and consistency were not the defining characteristics of the mackerel fisheries. The mackerel shoals originated in the Atlantic and arrived off the south and west coasts of Ireland in two distinct movements. The spring mackerel shoals usually arrived early in March. However, time and location of arrival were subject to variation due to ecological factors such as

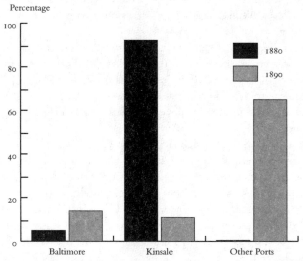

4. Percentage of total national landings by volume 1880 and 1890.

wind direction and water temperature. Fish stocks could also be affected by destructive fishing methods. One of the factors attributed to the collapse of the American mackerel fishery in 1888 was the killing of immature fish in previous seasons.[25] Ironically, this created a demand in America for mackerel that were caught and salted in the autumn along the south and west coasts of Ireland. This became known as the Autumn Mackerel Fishery. Baltimore made a modest start in 1888 with the export of 244 barrels (439 cwts.) worth £110.[26] Nature also dictated the movements of the sail-driven fishing fleet which could be equally immobilised by either calm or stormy weather conditions. The capital investment in large offshore boats allied to the unpredictability of the mackerel movements and the weather, therefore, made mackerel fishing a high-risk business.

However, the financial rewards could be high. Fr Davis claimed that eight Manx built fishing smacks built for Cape Clear fishermen costing £500 each earned £500 per crew of eight during the 1880 season.[27] The Rev. Green[28] observed in 1888 that the Irish spring mackerel were 'very large, from two and a half to three pounds each, and fetch nearly twice the price in Billingsgate of the mackerel caught on the English coast'.[29] This statement, however, disguises the fluctuating nature of the prices of the spring mackerel landed at Baltimore. In 1883, for instance, the prices per cwt. for mackerel landed at Baltimore and the other ten ports varied from 30.3 pence to 62.5 pence.[30] Factors such as buyers' cartels, transport costs to England, and competition in the English market place itself, which influenced price changes will be discussed later. Another important consideration was the vulnerability of the spring fishery because it was almost exclusively dependent on the English export market.[31]

Another potential source of instability for Baltimore was its lack of self-reliance in the supply of mackerel landings. Even though Fr Davis claimed that 'A few years ago not a single mackerel boat hailed from this harbour' and that the fleet had increased to twenty boats in 1881, the local boats were still in a minority among the fishing fleet landing mackerel in Baltimore during the spring season.[32] Of the 249 Irish vessels engaged in the mackerel fishery off the coast of Cork and Kerry during 1881, only forty-three were from the Skibbereen district whereas 157 came from the north and east coasts of Ireland. The national fleet itself, despite increasing from seventy vessels in 1870 to 249 in 1881, was outnumbered overwhelmingly by its international counterparts, as shown below where the composition of the total spring mackerel fleets on the south coast in 1881 is outlined:[33]

The 'causal wave-train'[34] of circumstances which had induced what might be termed the migratory fishing vessels to abandon Kinsale in favour of

English/Manx	French	Scotch	Irish	Total
357	111	20	249	737
48.4%	15.1%	2.7%	3.3%	100%

Baltimore in 1880 could equally change in favour of other ports and endanger Baltimore's burgeoning mackerel industry. This in turn could jeopardise the renewal of the town itself with which it was inter-linked. No such pessimism preoccupied Fr Davis when he endorsed the optimistic view of Baltimore's future expressed in the 1881 fishery report. However, in 1883 a contemporary critic of Fr Davis's optimism pithily conveyed the volatile nature of Baltimore's fishing industry with the remark that 'the fishing trade was transitory and evanescent'.[35]

An analysis of the annual statistical returns provided by the Inspectors of Irish Fisheries for mackerel landings between 1880 and 1911 in Figure 5 reveals that the volume and value of landings of mackerel both at a national and a local level were characterised by fluctuations with peaks and troughs that varied in duration and rate.[36] The founding of the Congested Districts Board in 1891 led to a new native west coast mackerel fishery which contributed to the decline of Baltimore and Kinsale but compensated on a national scale for the decrease in landings of mackerel by foreign fishing fleets at south coast ports from the 1890s onwards. Accordingly, the overall national trend for the thirty-two year period appears steady in Figure 5 despite the fluctuating nature of the volume of landings on an annual basis.

At a local level, the fluctuations in the volume of mackerel landings reflect the national pattern but do not necessarily replicate them in timing, duration

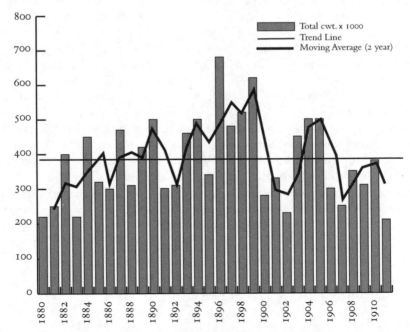

5. National total mackerel landings by volume 1880–1911

or rate. We can see, for instance, from Figure 6 that the period of greatest growth for Baltimore's mackerel industry was concentrated between 1880 and 1890 when 48.7 per cent of the total landings for the thirty-two year period took place. This contrasts sharply with the national peak which came later in 1898. A spectacular 296.2 per cent increase from 22,387 cwts.[37] in 1900 to 88,696 cwts. in 1901 failed to reverse the downward trend of mackerel landings at Baltimore. This was at variance with the overall stability of the national trend.

In evaluating the degree of fluctuation which the annual values of the total mackerel landings for Ireland experienced between 1880 and 1911 in Figure 7 it is important to recall that the 1880 value reflects the spring mackerel returns for Baltimore and Kinsale only. By 1890, however, the total value of mackerel landings for Ireland reached a peak of £212,672 for the thirty-two year period and represented the spring mackerel returns for twenty-two ports (mostly in Cork and Kerry)[38] and autumn mackerel returns for a variety of ports in counties Cork, Kerry, Clare, Mayo, and Donegal.[39] While the total volume of mackerel landings did not peak for another eight years (1898) as the west coast fishery expanded, the total value of these landings did not show a corresponding increase. Thus 'a tolerably good supply of fish and low prices' epitomised the volatility of the mackerel industry.[40]

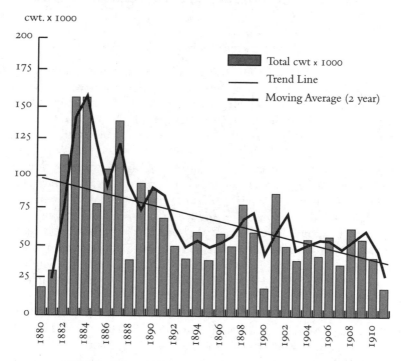

6. Baltimore total mackerel landings by volume 1880–1911

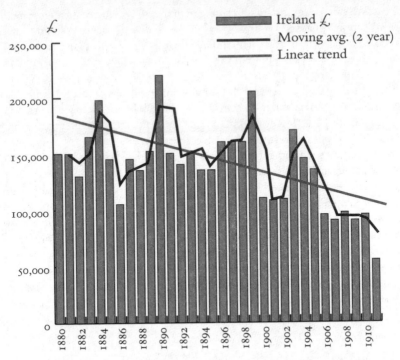

7. National total mackerel landings by value 1880–1911

An analysis of the annual landings of mackerel at Baltimore over the thirty-two year period has revealed that the success of the industry between 1880 and 1890 was not maintained. The dominant influence in this short-lived prosperity was a decrease in the average price per cwt. of fish landed at Baltimore over the thirty-two year period (see Figure 8) rather than a decrease in the volume of fish landed.[41]

Price itself was the product of the complex interplay between the weather, the movements of the mackerel, fishing practices and market forces. Increasing competition in the supply of fish to both the English and American markets reduced demand for Irish mackerel and led to a consequent drop in prices. The advent of steam propulsion and the return of the mackerel shoals to English waters enabled the new steam drifters fishing out of Milford to gain direct and 'rapid access to the inland cities'[42] of Manchester, Birmingham, Oldham and Sheffield which had hitherto been the principal destinations for Irish spring mackerel.[43]

Thus by the end of the 1880s, vessels from the international spring mackerel fleets, which had been the mainstay of Baltimore's brief but influential fishing boom, were increasingly bypassing Baltimore. Mackerel continued to arrive in Irish waters but falling prices proved a disincentive for fishermen both locally and nationally.[44] Baltimore's dependency on the

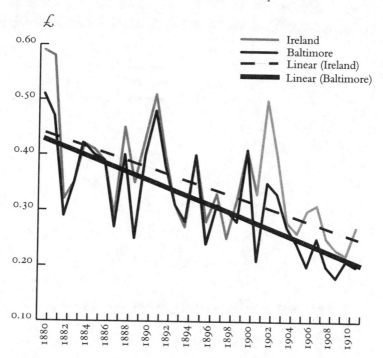

8. Average price per cwt. of total mackerel landings Ireland, Baltimore, 1880–1911

international markets of England and America for selling the mackerel and the failure to develop a home market on the same scale ensured that the dynamics of market forces in these places prevailed over the fluctuations of fish stocks and the limitations of the fishing fleet at a local level.

The spring mackerel fishery supplied fresh mackerel packed in ice to the English market. It was exported directly by steamers from Baltimore and other ports of landing or from Cork and Dublin to which it had been transported by train.[45] Conversely, the Autumn season began in 1887 with the sudden collapse of the American mackerel fishery in 1886.[46] The fish was cured and exported in barrels via Liverpool to America.[47] To provide an insight into the economic benefits of the mackerel industry for Baltimore and the surrounding area, the spring and autumn seasons will be examined separately (see Figure 9).

The spring mackerel fishery season in Baltimore extended over twelve weeks from March to June. The date for the commencement and conclusion of fishing was contingent on a number of variables, not least of which was the weather. The mackerel shoals usually arrived from the west close to 17 March but strong cold easterly winds, for instance, were blamed for delaying the shoals until as late as 8 April in Baltimore for the 1892 season.[48] Conversely, the *Eagle* reported that the 'magnificent' weather in early March 1883 precipitated an early start to the mackerel season.[49]

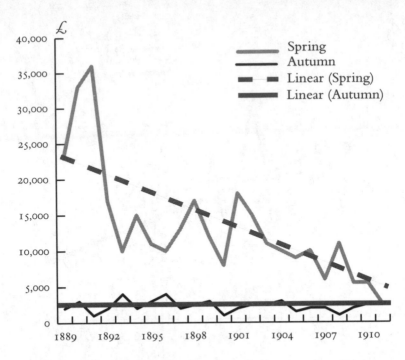

9. Baltimore spring and autumn mackerel landings by value 1889–1911

The competitive nature of the mackerel industry was based on the superior prices which Irish spring mackerel secured on the English market early in the season, as it was the only fresh fish available at that time of the year. This is illustrated by the following example of the average prices for spring mackerel landed at Baltimore during the 1894 season:[50]

The spring mackerel industry in Baltimore, as in other fishing centres, was primarily for the English market, despite the fruitless efforts of Fr Davis and Mr. Carey of the Baltimore Fishery Company to develop a market for fresh mackerel in the interior of Ireland.[51] It is not surprising, therefore, that the purchasing of the fresh mackerel at Baltimore and its transport to England was largely in the hands of English fish buyers who took up residence in the town for the duration of the season, thus contributing to the local economy through their living expenses.[52] They competed with local companies such as the Baltimore Fishery Company. English buyers were sometimes of forming a

March	April	May	June
23s.	25s.	10s.4d.	10s.

cartel to lower fish prices as was revealed in a Crime Branch Special Report of 26 October 1894.[53]

However, the buyers, both English and local, played a pivotal role in the stability of the local economy. This depended on a delicate balance between the supply of mackerel, the suitability of Baltimore as a landing and distribution centre and the demand for spring mackerel in England. The buyers were required to make a considerable capital investment over and above paying the fishermen in order to ensure that the mackerel arrived in England in marketable condition.[54] This, for example, in 1889 included the importation of 1,600 tons of ice from Norway, the rental of seven hulks anchored in the harbour for the storage of the ice and the chartering of eleven steamers for transporting the fresh mackerel to England.[55]

Accordingly, apart from providing the fishing fleet of 148 Irish, sixty-four Manx, fourteen English vessels based in Baltimore during the 1889 season with a market worth £22,000, the buyers also provided remunerative employment opportunities for people in the locality. £3,200, for example, was earned in twelve weeks by local men for shore-based work relating to preparing 86,000 cwts. of mackerel for the English market in 1889.[56] Though remunerative, the unstable nature of this income is revealed when it dropped to £2,800 in 1890 after fish landings at Baltimore decreased to 81,131 cwts.[57]

A picture of the harbour operations of the spring mackerel industry in Baltimore can be created from a more detailed examination of the 1890 season. Thus, the twenty-two fish buyers based in Baltimore for the season, employed 154 men at a rate of £1 5s. a week each in twenty-two fast rowing boats.[58] They met the incoming fishing boats before they reached port.[59] The buyers in competition with each other purchased the fish, as was the custom, on the water and not at the quay side.[60]

Fr Davis highlighted the remunerative nature of the fishery labour which paid £1 5s. a week in contrast with a figure of 5s. a week for agricultural labour.[61] Twenty-eight other men, known as 'packers', were engaged at £1 10s. a week to transfer the fish to the hulks in which the ice for packing the fish in boxes was stored.[62] A total of 2,410 tons of ice was imported from Norway in 1890[63] and stored in eight hulks moored in Baltimore harbour.[64] The decline of the spring mackerel trade with England in later years was marked by a progressive reduction in the importation of ice so that by 1911 only one hulk was needed to store 500 tons of ice when fish landings of 13,830 cwts. represented a 73 per cent drop on the 1890 figure.[65]

The perishable nature of the fresh mackerel and the claim (though exaggerated) that there was 'not a hamlet in England that the Irish mackerel does not go to'[66] encouraged the rapid transit of the iced mackerel to England. The introduction of steam-powered transport vessels or steamers, when most fishing vessels were wind-dependent, in the Kinsale mackerel fishery in 1867 had successfully fulfilled this function.[67] The steamer seemed ideal for the

Baltimore fishery in view of its fine harbour and comparative closeness to Milford,[68] the favoured port for the distribution of mackerel from Baltimore to London, Birmingham, Manchester and Liverpool and other English cities.[69] The inspectors of Irish fisheries stated in the 1891 annual report that it was 'the interest of buyers to keep as far east as possible, and so lessen the expense in steamers for dispatching the fish to the English markets'.[70]

The twenty-two steamers, however, that were chartered in 1890 to carry the fish to England cost £250 to £550 a month.[71] Only the buyers could afford this capital outlay when we consider that the earnings, excluding expenses, for a mackerel boat belonging to the Baltimore Fishery School during the 1890 season was a maximum of £377 9s.[72] These buyers were seasonal visitors to Baltimore. Changes in the supply of spring mackerel to England eventually made it more profitable for the fish merchants to remain in England. There was a consequent decline in steamer traffic to England from twenty-two in 1890 to five in 1900 and only one in 1910 and 1911.

The control of the steamers by the English buyers was regarded even in 1890 as a monopoly situation that put local involvement in the spring mackerel industry at a disadvantage.[73] It was also argued that the extension of the railway from Skibbereen to Baltimore in May 1893 would counteract this.[74] Previous to 1893, the alternative system of transporting the fish eight or nine miles to Skibbereen railway station by road or by the river Ilen (depending on the state of the tide) was slow and laborious and hardly ideal for a perishable commodity like fresh mackerel.[75] The major disincentive to using the railway was that the through rates to England were regarded as excessive to the extent that, when fish was cheap, the income was insufficient to even pay the rates.[76] In 1887 it cost 3s. per box to send mackerel directly to London by steamer whereas it cost three times as much, namely, 9s. per box, for fish from Baltimore to London via Cork and Milford.[77]

Just as spring mackerel landings of 140,912 cwts. worth £38,269 in 1887 marked the end of a seven year period of remarkable growth for Baltimore, the virtual collapse of the American mackerel industry spawned a new export trade of cured autumn mackerel to the United States of America.[78] Ironically, Baltimore's first small export consignment in 1888 of 439 cwts. of cured mackerel in 244 barrels (1 barrel = 1.8 cwts.) valued at £110 coincided with a 72.8 per cent decline in the volume of spring mackerel landings which amounted to 38,232 cwts. (valued at £17,566). The previous statistical analysis has shown that over the period 1888 to 1911 the spring mackerel landings in Baltimore, despite their downward trend, were superior both in volume and value to the autumn landings. Nevertheless, the contribution of the autumn mackerel landings to the economy of Baltimore deserves consideration.

Rev. W.S. Green stated in 1887 that the local consumption of fresh fish was extremely limited, adding that the consumption of salt fish and dried fish was much greater.[79] A survey in 1887 by the Inspectors of Irish Fisheries revealed the neglected and underdeveloped state of fish curing in Ireland.[80] There were only three private or commercial curers, rather than the fishermen themselves, in Ireland and Baltimore was not included.[81] However, many of the coastal fishing communities, including the Cape Clear fishermen, cured fish, including autumn mackerel, for their own consumption and for sale on a small scale in local markets.[82] The limited commercial value of this Irish cured fish in 1887 was attributed, in particular, to inferior methods of curing whereby it was not uncommon for Irish fishermen to 'salt the fish in their cabins . . . in such an unscientific manner that the fish could not command a market on a large scale'.[83] Perhaps it is not surprising then that approximately £200,000 of cured cod, ling and herring were imported into Ireland annually from Norway, Scotland and the Shetlands.[84]

The arrival in 1887 of American fish merchants, offering attractive prices to West Cork fishermen for properly cured mackerel, provided the incentive for the fishing communities of the south and west coasts to establish a properly constituted cured mackerel industry.[85] Special steamers transported the barrels of mackerel to Liverpool from which they were transhipped to America, principally through the seaports of New York, Boston and Philadelphia.[86] Cured mackerel was almost exclusively eaten 'by the working and poorer classes of Americans'[87] and in 1900 increased sales were predicted in Chicago 'on account of the large Catholic population and the increasing price of meat'.[88]

Coincidentally, the Baltimore Fishery School was opened on the 23 August 1887 by Baroness Burdett-Coutts. The trustees responded to the challenge of the new American market by initiating the building of a purpose built curing house and a programme of training for the boys in approved curing methods. The first fruits of their labour, namely 237 barrels, were cured for the American market in 1888.[89] A second curing facility owned by the Baltimore and Skibbereen Fishing Company also commenced business with a remarkably modest output of seven barrels.[90] A third curing firm, referred to as Messrs Kelson,[91] went into production in 1889 and curing increased to 3,523 barrels. Despite a further increase to 3,779 barrels in 1890, the Inspectors of Irish fisheries were dissatisfied with the quality of the cured fish exported to America. Baltimore was singled out to illustrate 'that even the best cured mackerel sent from Ireland fell far short of being as good as those imported from Norway, and that to become marketable the Irish-cured mackerel must be cured as well as the Norwegian'.[92]

The autumn mackerel season extended from August to November depending on the migration patterns of the mackerel and market fluctuations. The autumn industry differed from that of the spring. It was dominated by small boats as the autumn mackerel came close inshore where the bigger first-class boats sometimes could not shoot their nets.[93] Conversely, the spring mackerel tended to be further offshore which favoured the larger boats. Consequently, many of the island fishermen in the area were no longer dependent on

Baltimore for landing their autumn catches, unlike during the spring. Instead, Cape Clear, for instance, had its own curing facilities managed by both English buyers and local buyers such as Kieran Cotter who acted as agent for Sidney G. Gott of Birkenhead.[94] Mr. Gott in turn transhipped the cured mackerel from Liverpool to the firm of Messrs. Levins, fish merchants, Philadelphia.[95] Other English buyers, of course, including Petrie and Company, also had representatives in Baltimore along with local buyers such as Thomas Salter.[96]

Fortunately for the Baltimore economy, it suited a fleet of large fishing boats to fish out of Baltimore as some of the autumn mackerel shoals in the area tended to remain three to four miles offshore.[97] Thus in 1890 of the fleet of 104 vessels, ninety-two were first class and only twelve were second class.[98] The autumn fleet was also dominated by 80 Irish first class boats compared to 12 boats from the Isle of Man. This is in marked contrast with the larger and more cosmopolitan nature of the 1890 spring fleet, conveyed by the composition of the highest number of boats fishing in one day off Baltimore out of a fleet of 180 vessels as shown below:[99]

The limited involvement of foreign boats in the autumn fishery in Baltimore and the growth of local curing stations in competition with it ensured that Baltimore was never as important as a landing place for autumn mackerel as it was for spring mackerel. However, apart from being remunerative for the fishermen, and the people of Baltimore town and district, the curing of the autumn mackerel encouraged the development of a range of skills and onshore services conducive to an industrial rather than a subsistence economy.

The autumn mackerel, though of the same family, was regarded as more suitable for curing than the spring mackerel.[100] The perishable nature of mackerel and market requirements dictated how the fish was handled after the fish buyers had purchased it in Baltimore. The time constraints on the delivery of the spring mackerel in a fresh condition to England were solved by ice and fast transport. Freshness was also an imperative in the curing process of autumn mackerel exported to America, even if the speed of delivery to the market was not as crucial. This is graphically portrayed by Rev. W. S. Green who remarked that the mackerel was 'brought in the morning, at say 7 o'clock ... and it ought to be in the pickle before 4 o'clock in the day ... In fact the highest class of fish, which fetches the highest price, is that which is cured, split, and bled almost before the life is out of it'.[101]

This was a the first stage of the curing process but the actual sequence was: firstly, the mackerel was split which entailed cutting the fish down the back and removing the head and entrails. After the split fish was thoroughly washed,

Irish	Manx	English	French	Total
60	30	25	4	119
50.4%	25.2%	21.0%	3.4%	100.0%

the curing involved placing the fish between layers of salt in a barrel into which the pickle (a mixture of water and salt) was poured. After ten days in the pickle, 210 lbs. of cured fish was repacked into each shipping barrel which contained fresh salt and pickle. Further adjustments had to be made to the barrel before it was ready for the long voyage to America via Liverpool.[102]

Apart from the initial urgency to prepare the fish, the curing of the autumn mackerel was a protracted process that required a range of skills much in excess of what was required for icing the spring fish. It was a labour-intensive business whose value to the Cape Clear community is expressed by Conchúr Ó Síocháin: 'There wasn't a woman, a girl or a child in the Island who couldn't earn something in those days; and there was often so much to do that the very fishermen themselves had to lend a helping hand ... '.[103] The *Eagle* of 23 May 1893 praised a Mr. George W. Butler of Gloucester, Mass., a buyer of autumn mackerel at Baltimore where for years 'he affords such large and remunerative employment to many a poor family ... from Glandore to Baltimore.' In more prosaic but precise terms the inspectors of Irish fisheries' annual report of 1889 communicates the value of the autumn fishery to the shore-based labour force at Baltimore: £2,500 was paid in wages for a season that lasted from August to November. Apart from the thirty men employed in the buyers' boats at 18s. to £1 a week, there were 108 men, sixty-eight women and eighty-five boys employed in curing 3,523 barrels of fish. The men and women received approximately 18s. a week in wages while the boys were paid 12s. a week.

The curing industry must have been even more remunerative in the peak years of 1893 and 1896 when barrels of cured mackerel, totalling 5,085 and 5,146 respectively were exported from Baltimore.[104] The introduction of spring mackerel curing for the American market extended the curing season. Thus 801 barrels of spring mackerel were cured in Baltimore for the American market in 1892. Despite the overall decline, particularly from 1897 in the autumn mackerel industry, it still continued to make a substantial contribution to the income of both the fishermen and shore-based labour-force of Baltimore and the surrounding district.

As a result of these developments, Baltimore became one of the leading centres of the spring and autumn mackerel industry. An analysis of the mackerel landings over an extended period and the manner in which the mackerel industry evolved demonstrated the fragile base on which the industry was built. A 'sensitivity to external factors',[105] such as a dependency on outsiders to catch and market the fish (despite the emergence of a local fishing fleet), made Baltimore vulnerable to fluctuating prices in a highly competitive market where competition escalated rapidly in the 1890s.

Baltimore's Maritime Renaissance

Baltimore's contiguity to the fishing grounds and the spaciousness of its harbour facilitated its development from 1879 onwards as a centre for an expanding mackerel fleet during the fishing season. Its natural advantages, however, contrasted with the inadequacies of its man-made facilities for the landing and distribution of the mackerel for export to England, the limitations of the local fishing fleet and the need for a shore based industry to process the fish and service the fishing fleet. The well equipped fishing vessels of the international mackerel fleet based at Baltimore for the fishing season dominated the mackerel landings at Baltimore by virtue of their technical and numerical supremacy. However, in 1879 the local fishermen, beginning with the fishermen of Cape Clear (rather than the fishermen of Baltimore itself), through the financial support of Baroness Burdett-Coutts and leadership of Fr Davis, as explained in section one, began to modernise and expand the local fleet in emulation of their foreign counterparts.

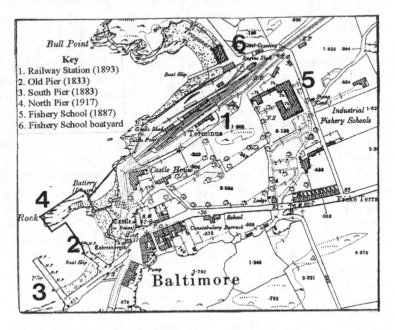

10. Infrastructural development relating to mackerel industry 1879–1917
(adapted from O.S. Co. Cork, 1:2500 sheet, CL 9)

Consequently, by 1886 the Cape Clear fleet consisted of eighteen vessels of 'as fine a model and as well equipped and as well mannered as any on the ocean'.[1] A Cape Clear fisherman was reputed to be the first in Ireland to use a steam-assisted winch to haul his nets.[2] Nevertheless, both vessels and equipment were imported from the Isle of Man, Scotland and England. Fr Davis claimed that even in 1886 there was not a single net-making machine in Ireland and within a 100 miles of Baltimore there was not a single person competent to make a sail for a first-class boat.[3] This was the context for the establishment in 1887 of the Baltimore Fishery School whose aim was to teach 'every art connected with fishing, from the making of lines and nets to the building of vessels, curing of fish . . .'[4] Since the spring mackerel landed in Baltimore was almost exclusively exported fresh to England and was highly perishable, supplying this market required efficient and well developed transit facilities which did not exist in Baltimore in 1879 despite a fine natural harbour. A prime example of this was the town's only pier. Lewis's account of it in 1837[5] contrasts with the blunt criticism of it by the Inspectors of Irish Fisheries in 1879 who deemed it 'useless, as in a moderate S.E. gale boats could not remain; a new harbour much required'.[6] The pragmatic Fr Davis agreed with this verdict and proceeded to lobby with the Baltimore Fishery Company for the construction of a new fishery pier west of the 1833 pier.[7] His support 'on behalf of the occupiers and fishermen of Baltimore and the adjacent coast and islands'[8] highlights the importance which he attached to the development of the fishing industry for the local economy as opposed to the 'golden harvest the strangers gathered on our coasts'.[9] Central to this objective was a new infrastructure in Baltimore itself that would enable it to become the landing and distribution centre of a properly constituted mackerel fishing industry with ancillary industries such as fish curing, boatbuilding and netmaking.[10] Fishery inspector, Joseph Hayes, in his official report on 8 July 1880, enthusiastically supported the application by Fr Davis and the Baltimore Fishery Company for a new fishery pier. He agreed that the existing pier had been adequate up to 1879 but that the 'forty to eighty large mackerel boats' which had chosen Baltimore as their base were unable to approach it at low water.[11] The mackerel fishery was dependent on large sail driven boats of fifteen tons or more and usually not less than forty-five feet in length as the spring mackerel were usually caught in deep Atlantic waters and the perishable catch and competitive market required speedy landing.[12] Permission for the construction of the new fishery pier which provided employment for twenty-four men[13] was granted by the Board of Trade on 6 December 1880.[14] This pier may be seen as the forerunner of major structural changes in Baltimore linked to the development of the mackerel industry and the leadership of Fr Davis. It was completed in the spring of 1883 under the direction of the Board of Works at a cost of £4,000.[15]

The narrow southern entrance to Baltimore Harbour, while shielding the harbour from Atlantic gales, presented 'a considerable risk' to fishermen approaching it from seaward 'on dark, stormy nights due to the absence of a guiding.[16] The increasing number of fishing boats using the harbour from 1879 onwards convinced the Fishery Commissioners of 'the importance of the port and its fisheries' and of the need to erect a light.[17] Fr Davis was equally convinced and the arrival in Baltimore on Tuesday 29 January 1883 of the vessel *Imogen* with representatives of the Commissioners of Irish Lights to choose a site[18] for the new lighthouse on Barrack Point, Sherkin Island, was attributed to the 'perseverance' of Fr Davis.[19] An even greater degree of perseverance allied to an unshakeable confidence in Baltimore's status as a fishing port was exhibited by Fr Davis in his successful campaign to establish the Baltimore and Skibbereen Harbour Board despite attempts by the Skibbereen representatives to exclude Baltimore.[20] The jurisdiction of the Harbour Board, established by act of Parliament on 24 June 1884, extended from the open sea at Baltimore and up the river Ilen to Skibbereen.[21]

The knowledge that poor boys from some of the coastal communities of Ireland were 'wandering about, idle, uneducated and half fed, open to temptations of the worst kind' had prompted Sir Thomas Brady, inspector of Irish fisheries, as early as 1871, to suggest a unique solution to Sir John Lentaigne, inspector of industrial schools in Ireland.[22] Sir Thomas recommended the use of training ships to educate these young boys in the skills and trades relating to sea fishing. Even in 1885, fourteen years later, the vision of these two men had still not been fulfilled but the developing spring mackerel industry was bringing 'comparative prosperity' to the fishing communities of the south west, and in particular to Baltimore. This was reflected in new and improved boats in an expanding local fleet led by the Cape Clear fishermen with funding from the Burdett-Coutts fund and the leadership of Fr Davis. Another clergyman, the Catholic bishop of Ross, Dr. Fitzgerald, had entered into a correspondence in August 1885 with Sir John and the chief secretary for Ireland, Sir William Hart-Dyke regarding the establishing of an industrial school for boys in his diocese.[23] Sir John, in a memo to the chief secretary on 9 September 1885, advocated implementing Sir Thomas' original proposal of a school 'for training boys for fishing purposes' located at Baltimore rather than on a training ship.[24] Sir John favoured Baltimore in view of the progress of the fishing trade in the district through the benevolence of Baroness Burdett-Coutts.

A deputation consisting of Dr. Fitzgerald, Sir John, Fr Davis, and Sir Thomas visited the chief secretary, Sir William Hart-Dyke on 7 October 1885.[25] Arising out of this meeting, it was decided to build a school at Baltimore which would be certified under the Industrial Schools Act (Ireland), 1868.[26] This would enable the school to secure an annual capitation grant of £13 for each boy but it would not include any financial provision for the

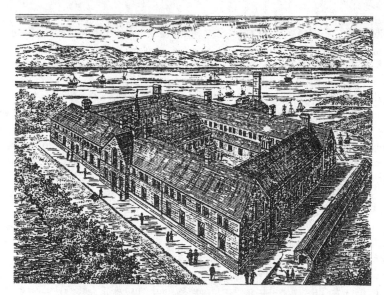

11. Baltimore Fishery School (courtesy Dept. of Education)

building or equipping of the new school.[27] Under the terms of the Act, only destitute or neglected boys between the ages of six and sixteen years would be accommodated in the school. Though these boys would be 'committed' to the school after being summoned before a magistrate, Fr Davis was adamant that they 'must be destitute but not criminal'.[28]

Baltimore Fishery School, however, would differ from all other industrial schools because of the aspirations of the founders of the school to foster the development of the fishing industry by 'training boys in trades connected with the capture and curing of fish'.[29] In addition to this, it was intended to confine entry to 150 boys drawn from all the maritime districts of Ireland. The tension between the requirements in relation to the revival of the fishing industry and the restrictions imposed by the Industrial Schools Act were reflected from the outset in the designation of the new dual purpose institution. Whereas the trustees of the school chose to refer to it as both 'The Baltimore Industrial School' and 'Industrial Fishing School, Baltimore' when making a public appeal for funds August 25, 1887,[30] it was officially incorporated as 'Baltimore Fishery School' on October, 1889.[31]

With remarkable speed, Dr. Fitzgerald, Sir John, Fr Davis, and Sir Thomas acting as trustees, leased a site for the new school from the trustees of the Carbery estate at a annual rent of £25 for ninety-nine years.[32] The site overlooked the harbour and sloped down to an inlet known as Tragunarin at the north east corner of the harbour.[33] With no obvious funding but in the expectation of raising money through appeals to both government and private sources, the trustees contracted Mr. John Sisk of Cork to erect the new school.

The school would be built in stages. The first stage which provided accom-modation for 75 boys cost £3,000. A grant of £1,000 from the Grand Jury of County Cork, and a sum of £561 6s. 4d. from the M'Comas Bequest and numerous private contributions ensured an initial financial independence but obscured a dependency on private rather than state funding.[34]

Accordingly, the responsibility of the trustees for raising money to build the new fishery school did not at first appear as onerous as it would later become. However, it became apparent at an early stage that the dual functions of the new fishery school would require resources of a human, financial, and material nature beyond the scope of the conventional industrial school structure. Consequently, an application by the trustees to Mr. Balfour, the chief secretary, for a grant in aid of £10,000 stressed that the new institution would be built and equipped as a centre of maritime industry and technical knowledge in a way that Fr Davis believed the industrial schools had 'never been used before'.[35]

The £10,000 was specifically sought 'to add to the buildings already erected and erect plant necessary for instruction in and the prosecution of the various branches of the fishery trade'.[36] A detailed breakdown of the expenditure necessary to fulfil the above plan proposed an outlay of £8,260 on structural projects such as curing houses and workshops and the purchase of two fishing vessels and equipment, including net making machines.[37] The proposal also envisaged a further £1,080 to pay for a general manager and a team of instructors with specialist skills that varied from boatbuilding to fish curing.

The trustees emphasised how the new fishery school could impart to the young boys the skills necessary for future employment, but unlike in the conventional industrial schools, it would be conducted in the context of a commercial enterprise. This unique alliance of educational training with commercial enterprise was the basis of the trustees' belief that the Baltimore Fishery School would become a 'centre of industry and of technical knowledge for the whole coast population of Ireland'.

The high expectations of the trustees for the Baltimore Fishery School were endorsed by the Baroness Burdett-Coutts who agreed to officially open the school on 17 August 1887.[38] The baroness and her husband, William Burdett-Coutts M.P., who had become a trustee of the school, each donated £100 to a fund for further development of the school.[39] The founding of the Baltimore Fishery School was perceived as a product of the benevolence of the baroness to the people of Baltimore district over the preceding period of twenty-five years. Baltimore's example inspired the wish in 1887 that 'in a short time the neglected coasts will contain more than one Baltimore'.[40] With Baltimore cast as a role model for the fishing communities of Ireland, the ceremony and publicity associated with the opening of the new Fishery school served to elevate the school to the status of an icon of a developing native Irish fishing industry. Over seventy Irish and English newspapers and other publications carried glowing reports which bordered on hyperbole.[41] The regal arrival of

Baroness Burdett-Coutts in the steam yacht, *The Pandora*, and the praise for both herself and Fr Davis, dominated the description of the many dignitaries present among whom was the archbishop of Cashel, Dr. Croke.[42] Sir Thomas Brady, despite being one of the original founders, did not share the limelight.

The acclaim which the Baltimore Fishery School had received at its opening and the optimism about its future role in the development of Irish fishing industry was not reciprocated by the government in the letter of 22 September 1887.[43] This informed Fr Davis, now acting as manager of the school, that parliament was restricting its contribution to £5,500, despite a request by the trustees for a grant of £10,000. It seems, however, that the indefatigable Fr Davis was happy to regard it as an interim payment to enable the trustees to press ahead with their plans for further expansion.[44]

Thus the school was ready to accommodate the first group of forty-five boys by November 1887.[45] These boys were chosen from existing industrial schools to provide 'a nucleus of trained boys' before the 'outside boys' (untrained in the discipline of an industrial school) were admitted.[46] A total of seventy-five boys were in residence at the end of the year. It seems that the need to establish an institutional routine boys from coastal communities. It was only on 26 March 1889 that Fr Davis was able to state that 'we will in future confine ourselves in our selection of boys to the coast districts'.[47] Already the association of destitute boys with the new fishery school was proving a disincentive in coastal communities. He also admitted that it would accordingly 'take some months' before its maximum intake of 150 boys would be reached. A year later numbers had increased to 100 boys but eventually by 1891 the school was accommodating 150 boys aged between six and sixteen years, after additional accommodation had been provided at a cost of £2,000.[48]

Apart from complying with the requirements of the Industrial Schools Act of 1868, the management and functioning of Baltimore Fishery School was governed by the Educational Endowments (Ireland) Act, 1885 which came into force on 30 October 1889.[49] Henceforth, Dr. Fitzgerald, Roman Catholic bishop of Ross, Fr Davis, parish priest of Baltimore, and a representative of the Carbery estate and the successors of each of the three parties would be ex-officio members of the governing body. This body, apart from governing and managing the school, would be entitled to co-opt four other governors for a four year term. Ironically, Sir Thomas Brady joined the governing body as a co-opted member despite having pioneered the project.

Fr Davis pressed on with his twin objectives. Firstly, he had to ensure that the usual industrial school accommodation and education system would be provided for the full quota of 150 boys. Secondly, facilities had to be put in place for training the boys in all aspects of fishing, both afloat and ashore, as a commercial enterprise. The concept of preparing the young boys of the fishery school for careers in the fishing industry in a commercial environment was not only educationally sound (and of national importance) but was also crucially important for the economic viability of the school. £38,000 worth of spring mackerel had been landed at Baltimore during the 1887 season but, despite an increasing local fleet, 'by far the larger proportion' was paid to English, Scotch, and Manx fishermen.[50] The trustees of the Baltimore Fishery School were determined that the school would earn its share of this 'golden harvest'[51] by fitting out its own fishing smacks. Each boat would employ four men assisted by two boys from the school. It was envisaged that three quarter's of the boats' receipts would go to the school. Meanwhile the boys would be 'learning the most improved mode of fishing' so that they would eventually leave the school as 'skilled fishermen'.[52] The learning of practical skills on the water would be complemented by shore based instruction in various aspects of seamanship such as navigation and the mending of sails and nets.

Fr Davis expressed satisfaction at the progress of the school in his manager's report for 1890. He referred in particular to the 'remunerative prices' received for nets manufactured in the school and the 'three tons of ling and cod' caught by the boys for consumption in the school. However, he made it clear that the primary function of the school to produce 'expert fishermen' was being frustrated by insufficient capital and by the obligation to discharge boys at the age of sixteen.[53] His report shows that, even though the mackerel fishing was the most lucrative industry, only eight boys out of a total enrolment of 150 were engaged in fishing aboard four first class boats.

The physical demands of working aboard a sail-driven mackerel boat in Atlantic waters sometimes constituted 'sheer slavery' as described by fisherman, Conchúr Ó Síocháin. He claimed, for instance, that it 'took at least three hours to haul the train of nets on board'.[54] Atlantic gales not only added to the hardship but accounted, not infrequently, for the drowning of fishermen at sea.[55] William Bennett and John Byrne, two boys who were aboard fishing vessels of the school for the 1893 season, were commended for their 'pluck and bravery' during 'one of the severest gales ever experienced at sea'.[56] It is no wonder then that boys were required to be at least fourteen years of age before they could begin their training aboard a mackerel boat. Fr Davis and his successors sought unsuccessfully to have the age limit of sixteen years extended to eighteen as they felt it was not possible for the boys to be fully fledged fishermen at sixteen years.[57]

Newman in 1895 informs us that four fishery school vessels earned a total of £785 8s. 9d. during the spring mackerel season but £250 15s. 10d. in crew wages and an unspecified sum for their maintenance would have to be deducted from this income.[58] One boat, the Sir Edward Birkbeck, provided a profit of £101 16s. 10d. but expenses of £34 9s. 2d. had to be offset against it.[59] This twenty-three ton first class boat cost £900 and £700 was regarded as the minimum outlay for a first class fishing boat in 1894.[60] Lack of funds kept the school fleet in 1894 to five vessels which, at two boys per boat, severely curtailed its training programme. Inspector Blennerhassett recommended that 'at least ten to twenty vessels' be attached to the school which would enable a maximum of forty boys to be given a practical training. Nineteen boys, having reached the age of sixteen, were discharged in 1893 but only one boy, Stephen O'Donnell, took up fishing in Carna, County Galway with a further three boys opting for other seafaring occupations such as joining the navy.[61] However, one other boy named as Patrick Roche undertook employment as a net manufacturer in Musselburgh. Ironically, this coincided with the appointment of a fishery master.[62]

The publication of the governors' report for 1895 provoked the *Eagle* to regard the school as a having failed in its primary purpose of training boys to be 'scientific fishermen'.[63] Over a period of five years up to December 1895, 111 boys had been discharged. Even though thirty-five boys went into occupations of 'seafaring, fishing, net making and the navy', the newspaper suggested that few boys were actually engaged in fishing. This trend continued. The Inspector's report for 1911 reveals that, of the thirty boys discharged in 1911, only seven boys found employment as fishermen.[64] The remainder of the boys, according to the report, were engaged in occupations that typified those pursued by boys discharged from conventional industrial schools. There is no indication from the report as to whether any of these occupations, which included both skilled trades or non-skilled labour, had a marine dimension. However, one past pupil of the school, Tom Moynihan, became a master boat builder and foreman of the boatyard.

A further disappointment to the governors of the school was the shortage of admissions of boys from the maritime counties and particularly those from a seafaring background.[65] It was felt that these boys would be more amenable to learning modern piscatorial skills which they could in turn pass on to their own communities along the coast of Ireland. However, the procedure by which all boys admitted to the school had to be committed by a magistrate, seems to have been particularly unacceptable among many of the coastal communities because of the fear that they would be stamped 'with the seal of degradation'.[66]

Fr Davis highlighted what he termed the 'backward' state of the native Irish fishing industry when he lamented in June 1887 (two months before the school was opened) the shortage of professionally-run curing centres.[67] At the same time 10,000 tons of cured fish was being imported annually into Ireland according to Fr Davis and his fellow trustees.[68] The existence of a market for cured fish in Ireland convinced Fr Davis that it 'would be enormously remunerative' for the school to establish a curing facility in the school.[69] However, a much cherished ambition of Fr Davis to develop a market within Ireland for cured fish was not fulfilled during his lifetime.[70] In its place the opening up of an export trade of cured autumn mackerel from Ireland to America in 1888 coincided with the first year of the school's existence.

It is a tribute to the organisational skills of Fr Davis and the industry of the young curers that they were able to respond to this new market. In their first commercial curing venture, the boys of the Baltimore Fishery School cured

237 barrels (439 cwts.) of mackerel for the American market in 1888, as against seven barrels by the Baltimore and Skibbereen Company.[71] A year earlier Mr. R. Carey, representing the local fish-buying company in Baltimore, stated that 'tons of mackerel were going waste . . . for want of curing'.[72] It is not surprising, therefore, that there were initial problems with complaints about the quality of the cured fish.[73] A Mr. Goverstein from Norway was invited to Baltimore to provide instruction in the curing process because Norwegian methods of curing fish were regarded as superior.[74]

The description by Sir Thomas Brady in November 1896 of 'eighty boys daily curing fish for America, often at night on the shore by torch light till long after the hour they should have gone to rest', encapsulates the commercial nature of the school's activities.[75] Despite the fluctuating nature of the mackerel industry, curing mackerel for the American market provided modest but much needed revenue for the school which was struggling to be financially self-sufficient. In the six year period between 1889 and 1895, profit from 'the curing house', as it was termed, averaged £118 annually whereas netmaking and netmending suffered an annual loss of £187.[76] While acknowledging the commercial value of the mackerel curing, Inspector John Fagan in his report of 29 September 1899 questioned the long term educational value of 'the sloppy, soiling nature of the work'.[77]

By November 1896 it was becoming apparent that creating an infrastructure appropriate to the requirements of a fishery school demanded financial resources over and above those of the conventional industrial school. Apart from the usual accommodation and training facilities, the fishery school needed specialist facilities such as curing and boatbuilding sheds and the development of a boat launching area. Additional land had also been purchased so that the total area of land attached to the school in 1894 was fourteen acres.[78] Sir Thomas Brady, one of the founders, admitted in November 1896 that they had not yet achieved 'what the original founders intended' even though £9,000 had been spent on a building programme and the school had had 'the best year yet' in practical training for the fishing industry.[79] He attributed this to a lack of proper state funding and complained that 'we are expected to make bricks without straw'.

A major financial crisis in 1897 threatened the future of the school. At a board of governors' meeting of 26 October 1897, Dr. Kelly, bishop of Ross, advocated changing the management of the school because of 'the frightful waste that was going on'.[80] Inspector Blennerhassett was also critical of the school management but he did concede that the administration of the school under the Industrial Schools Act was inappropriate for a fishery school and presented 'insurmountable difficulties' for the governors of the school.[81] Though he recommended a radical overhaul of the working of the school, it continued to function under the restrictions of the industrial schools' system. An improvement in its financial affairs in 1899 coincided with the emerging and ultimately successful boatbuilding facility of Baltimore Fishery School.[82]

Despite a tradition of boatbuilding in Baltimore,[83] the funding provided by Baroness Burdett-Coutts in 1879 was largely spent on fishing boats imported from the Isle of Man. The governors of the school were determined to introduce boatbuilding as a source of employment for the boys and as a major contributor to a revival of the boatbuilding industry. Lack of funding, however, delayed until 1893 the appointment of an instructor in boatbuilding and carpentry.[84] The process of transforming boatbuilding from an educational activity to a commercial enterprise extended over another five years. Thus in 1898, the extension of an existing shed and slipway enabled the school to commence its first major boatbuilding contract which was worth £150.[85] This was commissioned by the Congested Districts Board for the building of a boat to be delivered to Galway for £10.[86]

Baltimore was included as a district of the Congested Districts Board when it was founded in 1891. The Congested Districts Board, as part of its programme of fishery development in the congested areas, financed the acquisition of sail-powered fishing boats built in Ireland, Scotland and the Isle of Man from 1896 onwards.[87] Dr. Kelly, bishop of Ross, at a meeting of the board of governors in September 1899, requested a grant from the Congested Districts Board for extending the slipway to facilitate the repair of fishing boats which hitherto were obliged to sail to distant boatyards, even in the Isle of Man. Dr. Kelly referred to Baltimore's status as a 'pioneer of mackerel fishing in recent times'. The Fishery School's increasing importance as a boatbuilding and repair centre was reflected in the construction of the new slipway and a new boat building-shed which was commenced in 1904.[88] Its commercial viability was endorsed by a grant from the Congested Districts Board and orders for new Congested Districts Board funded fishing boats.[89] Thus for instance, between 1901 and 1905 six nobbies were built, one of the smallest being the thirty-seven foot *Topaz*[90] built in 1899 for £130 and the largest being the forty-six foot *Opal (Gem)* which cost £333 in 1902. The school informed the Congested Districts Board in December 1904 that 'due to the amount of work in hand' it would be unable to accept the contract for building a zulu class fishing boat.[91] Six fishing boats, including four large deep-sea boats, were built in 1911.[92]

The *Cork Examiner* reported on 30 October 1912 that the boatyard had established a reputation for building boats 'combining speed, safety and durability'. We also learn from the report that increasing demand necessitated the building of another more sophisticated boatbuilding and repair facility at a cost of £2,000, 'every penny of which was borne by the schools'. This building was erected in time to build the seventy foot fishing vessel, *Carbery Queen*, whose completion in 1912 was an important innovation for the school.

The launch of the *Carbery Queen* in the spring of 1913 was the product of a design competition instituted by the Congested Districts Board for the building of three large fishing boats combining both engine and sail power. The competition and the building contract were won in the face of competition from Manx and Scotch boatyards which had for so long monopolised both the design and production of fishing boats for Irish fishermen. Central to this success was the design and construction skills of the foreman of the fishery school boatyard, Tom Moynihan,[93] who was a past pupil of the school, having entered 'as a little fellow and never working a day in any other institution.'[94]

Tom Moynihan had served his time under the previous foreman, Henry Skinner. After twenty years as foreman of the boatyard, Mr. Skinner left the Fishery School to establish his own boatyard closer to Baltimore village and beside the old pier. The launch, in April 1913, of the fifty-six foot motor fishing vessel, *Gabriel,* which he had designed and built in his new boatyard, followed closely on the launch of the *Carbery Queen.* These two new fishing vessels were the harbingers of a new era in which the sail would eventually make way for the engine while the market for Baltimore mackerel in England declined.

In February 1888 a comprehensive report on the sea fisheries of the south and south-west of Ireland, commissioned by the Fisheries Committee of the Royal Dublin Society, was issued. The author of the report, Rev. W.S. Green, highlighted the increasing catching power of the mackerel industry but emphasised how backward it still was in relation to the requirements of a market economy based, primarily, on an export trade to England. In particular, he pointed out the folly of 'encouraging the landing of vast quantities of fish, while the means of transit remain so imperfect that the mere catching of fish is an unprofitable business.'[95] Green regarded the development of the railway system and the reduction in transportation charges as the cornerstone of a transportation network that would offset the logistical and financial disadvantages of a distant market and a perishable product.

A campaign to extend the railway from Skibbereen to Baltimore was fortuitously facilitated by the Light Railway Act 1889, initiated by the chief secretary for Ireland, Arthur Balfour. Baltimore and other coastal communities along the Atlantic seaboard would at last be included in the remarkable expansion in post-Famine Ireland of the railway network, which was seen as a prerequisite for the development of a market-driven economy.[96]

A local government inquiry regarding the merits of the proposed railway extension to Baltimore was held at the Baltimore Fishery School in January 1890. Newspaper reports concentrated on the evidence of the chief witnesses at the enquiry, Fr C. Davis, fishery inspector Sir Thomas Brady and Mr. A. Gordon, traffic manager of the Cork Bandon and South Coast Railway.[97] These three men were unanimous in their advocacy of the merits of the proposed railway line, primarily to consolidate Baltimore's emergence as 'one of if not the most important fishing stations on the south coast'. Their evidence emphasised how this new-found success was underpinned by the strength of the mackerel industry. They contended that because of its value to the local economy, and the infrastructural developments such as the new pier and founding of the Baltimore Fishery School which it had stimulated, railway transit facilities were required in Baltimore to complement the use of steamers to transport the mackerel.

The eleven steamers[98] which had conveyed the spring mackerel directly from Baltimore to England for distribution to the large cities during the 1889 season would seem to have been a more suitable form of fish transport and in keeping with Baltimore's fine harbour and new pier. However, Fr Davis in his evidence maintained that the 'poor fishermen' sent a great deal of mackerel by rail, despite the difficulties of transporting it to the railhead at Skibbereen, as the economics of chartering steamers at '£200 to £400 a month' favoured the 'English fish buyers who lodged in Baltimore for the mackerel season'.[99]

Both Fr Davis and Sir Thomas Brady had already given evidence regarding the mackerel industry and related market distribution problems to the Royal Commission on Irish Public Works which had visited Baltimore in June 1887.[100] Sir Thomas Brady, himself, had demonstrated in a detailed submission that 'the rate of carriage for mackerel is about half its average market value, while that of butter is about one-fiftieth, and for fresh meat and poultry less than one-twentieth'.[101] While Sir Thomas prophetically declared that 'this great fishing trade was likely to collapse in the south of Ireland, if the expenses were not reduced',[102] the Commission agreed that 'the rates from the south-western district of Ireland appear to us unduly high' and placed Irish fishermen at a disadvantage when competing with their counterparts in England.[103] This complaint was reiterated by Rev.W.S. Green to the Vice-Regal Commission on Irish Railways in 1907.[104] Increased through rates to England in 1920 were blamed for the collapse of the mackerel trade with England.[105]

Another physical and financial disincentive to the carriage of mackerel by rail from Baltimore related to a peculiarity of the railways running into Cork from the west. The line to Cork, which was managed by the Cork and Bandon Railway Companies, had its terminus at Albert Quay and was not linked to the railway systems of the other companies, such as the Great Southern and Western on the north side of the city. 'Owing to this break the cost of carriage from the important and growing district of south-west Cork and the injury to the fish by delay and transhipment, are much increased, the cost of cartage alone through the city being 2s. per ton'.[106]

Through the Baltimore Extension Railway Order 1890, a government free grant of £56,700 was provided from public monies for the extension of the railway line from Skibbereen to Baltimore.[107] The plans for the new railway, however, excluded the provision of a new deep water pier and would require the transport of the fish over a quarter of a mile to the new railway terminus. The *Cork Examiner* of 6 August 1890 attributed government support for the new railway to Baltimore's importance as a fishery station, the founding of the Baltimore Fishery School, and to the 'appeals in high places' by Fr Davis among his 'influential friends'.

The same paper in a series of graphic reports described the potatoes along the south west coast as being 'miserable in size, in many cases 'black' and 'hardly eatable' after an exceptionally wet summer in 1890. In many areas, including Baltimore, the potato crop was regarded as the worst since 1879. The possibility of employment[108] on the new railway line between Baltimore and Skibbereen was regarded as fortuitous for the poorer people of the distressed districts, as it represented 'their only chance of keeping body and soul together during the winter'.[109] The alternative was 'an exodus to the workhouse' in Skibbereen.[110] Construction work on the new railway began in November 1890 and was scheduled for completion 31 March 1892.[111] Mrs Tuke, en route to Baltimore with her husband, James Hack Tuke, to visit Fr Davis 5 February 1891 observed men and boys working for 2s. a day on the new railway which she termed: 'one of the Government relief works'.[112]

The construction of the new railway, despite being dogged by delays, was nearing completion in December 1892.[113] However, the optimism which had preceded it among the people of Baltimore was being replaced by an increasing scepticism about its value to the fishing industry in the district without the building of a deep water pier connected to the new railway line. This was articulated in an editorial in the *Eagle* on 21 Jan 1893. The same article acknowledged that Fr Davis had 'never lost sight of the necessity for this pier, in order to make the railway a success' but 'with extraordinary tact and shrewdness' had merely postponed lobbying for the pier. The 'piecemeal'[114] strategy Fr Davis had adopted in relation to 'the deep water pier he had in view', [115] was nullified by his premature death at the age of sixty-three on 13 October 1892.[116] The support of the *Eagle* and the efforts of the Baltimore and Skibbereen Harbour Board in relation to the new pier were to no avail as the first official train steamed into the new Baltimore station on 2 May 1893.[117] Considering the spirited community based campaign for the new railway, it is not surprising that the 'remarkably cool reception . . . to a degree far below freezing point' which the first train received was termed 'a disgrace' by the *Eagle*.[118] The newspaper was particularly critical of the absence of those who stood to benefit most from the new rail service. It referred specifically to the landlord, Lord Carbery, and representatives of the fishing industry to which it referred as 'the great industrial enterprise centred in Baltimore'. The report attributed the success of this industry to the talents of Fr Davis and was pessimistic of its continued success without him.

Despite the absence of Fr Davis and the lack of a new pier, three wagons of mackerel were attached to the inaugural train when it steamed out of Baltimore at 1.15 p.m. on 2 May 1893.[119] This was recorded as the best catch of the spring mackerel season which had commenced on 4 April.[120] However, by the end of the month there were reports of general disillusionment with the new line which, without the new pier, was regarded as 'practically useless' for the fishing industry.[121] A report in the *Eagle* dismissed the incomplete railway line as 'an abortion'.[122] Of the 41,461 cwts. of mackerel landed in Baltimore during the 1893 spring and autumn seasons, only 1,510 cwts. were transported by the new railway.[123] Other fish, principally, salmon, trout and herring, sent by rail amounted to only seventy-three cwts.[124]

In 1894 the quantity of mackerel transported directly from Baltimore by rail increased to 6,030 cwts but it still represented only 10.2 per cent of a total of 59,174 cwts. of mackerel landed that year.[125] An examination of the figures over a longer duration, that is, the fifteen year period between 1893 to 1907, reveals that the 82,436 cwts. of mackerel sent by rail from Baltimore averaged only 11.3 per cent of the total mackerel landings of 731,939 cwts.[126] These figures were in sharp contrast with the optimistic forecast at the 1890 inquiry at Baltimore Fishery School, where estimates of 25 per cent to 50 per cent of the total landings were quoted.[127] Ironically, while the 33,920 cwts. of mackerel landed at Baltimore in 1907[128] was the lowest since 1881, the 13,523 cwts. sent by train, though representing 39.9 per cent of the total landings contrary to the fifteen year average, it did not match the 1890 expectations of 45,000 cwts. via the new railway.

In 1912 a new three quarter mile link across the river Lee was completed between the Cork terminus of the Baltimore line at Albert Quay to the Glanmire Road station north of the river.[129] While it eliminated the expense and difficulties of transhipment, it came too late. Similarly, on 17 December 1913, twenty years after the opening of the much criticised Baltimore Extension Railway in 1893, permission was finally given to Cork County Council for the construction of a deep water pier on to which the railway would be extended.[130] The approved plan was broadly similar to that prepared in 1894 and recommended strongly by an inspector of the Congested Districts Board on the basis of its importance for 'the development of a fresh fish trade'.[131] The new pier with its railway siding was finally completed in 1917 at a cost of £10,000 by the Congested Districts Board.[132]

The revival of the mackerel industry in 1879 contributed significantly to the rejuvenation of Baltimore's maritime infrastructure. Apart from improving Baltimore's natural advantages as a harbour for the landing and export of mackerel by building piers and a new lighthouse, its advantages as a mackerel distribution centre were enhanced by the extension of the railway from Skibbereen to Baltimore. The establishment of the Baltimore Fishery School represented an experimental venture in creating an indigenous maritime industrialisation related to the fishing industry in Baltimore itself. This in turn was intended as the prototype for similar ventures among Ireland's fishing communities. Despite the limited success of the Fishery School and the transience of the mackerel fisheries boom in Baltimore, the infrastructural developments which it spawned had a more enduring impact on the physical environment of Baltimore and the restoration of its maritime identity.

The Social and Political Impact of the
Baltimore Mackerel Industry

This section will consider the nature of the interaction between the natives of Baltimore and the islands on the one hand and the visiting fishermen, attracted by the mackerel, nomadic by profession and products of different social, political, and mental worlds. This period also saw an influx of newcomers attracted to Baltimore on a permanent basis by the employment and prosperity associated with the mackerel industry. The Baltimore Fishery School itself represented a community of newcomers radically different to the settled community and individual newcomers.

An examination of the census statistics from 1841 to 1911 reveals that the population of Baltimore town, despite some fluctuations, increased substantially during that period while the population of Baltimore townland fell (see Figure 12 above). It is notable that the post-Famine population of 189 people in Baltimore town in 1851 represented an increase of 12.5 per cent on

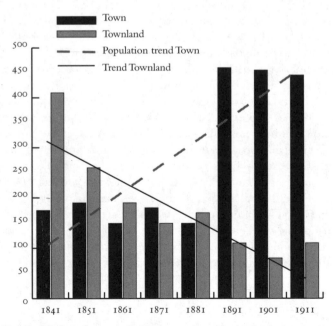

12. Population change in Baltimore town and townland 1841–1911

a population of 168 people in 1841. The townland of Baltimore during the same period experienced a decrease of 37.1 per cent from 412 people to 259 people. More noteworthy, however, is the period between 1881 and 1891 when the population of Baltimore town increased by 219.1 per cent from 146 to 466 people.[1] Meanwhile Baltimore townland receded further by 34.7 per cent from 173 to 113 people.[2] The Baltimore Fishery School itself which was opened in 1887 had a total of 160 people (composed of ten staff and 152 boys) in residence by 1891. This boosted the total population of Baltimore town, which was 146 people in 1881, by 109.6 per cent.

This coincided with Baltimore's emergence as one of the leading centres of the mackerel industry and was replicated in other fishing centres such as Castletownbere, even if 'fishing in county Cork . . . never served as a long term promoter of urban growth' unlike other urban centres in Atlantic Europe.[3] The population figure for Baltimore town remained stable until 1911 when a decrease of 4.9 per cent on the 1891 total was recorded. Meanwhile, the declining population of Baltimore townland plummeted further in 1901 by 31.9 per cent to 77 people but increased again by 55.8 per cent within ten years to a total of 120 people in 1911. A positive influence undoubtedly was the new Irish Land Act of 1903 which enabled the tenants of the Carbery Estates in the townland to purchase their holdings.[4]

Having charted the general movements of the population changes which both the town and townland of Baltimore experienced after the Famine to the eve of the 1914–18 War, a closer study will be made of what could be termed the 'demographic spring tide'[5] which impacted on Baltimore between 1881 and 1891. This was also the period of the greatest volume of mackerel landings which in turn acted as a catalyst for major economic, infrastructural and institutional developments. With Baltimore awash with people and mackerel, the question arises as to how the established community responded to an evolving demographic and economic milieu.

The employment opportunities afforded by the mackerel fisheries benefited not only the settled population but also attracted new people to Baltimore. The preparation of spring mackerel for export to England during the twelve week spring season was a labour intensive operation and much more remunerative than agricultural labouring. A resident population of 146 people in Baltimore in 1881 obviously required an influx of seasonal workers as landings of mackerel increased. 176 men, for instance, were employed in various capacities within the harbour during the spring mackerel season from March to July 1887.[6] The inception in 1888 of the curing of autumn mackerel for export to America provided further remunerative and extensive employment in Baltimore through the winter and by 1893 it had become a 'great industry at which so many hundred hands were employed'.[7]

However, the increasing employment from the fishing industry gave rise to complaints of overcrowding in Baltimore, particularly during the fishing season.[8] Mr. M. Evans Freke, while representing the Trustees of the Carbery Estates in a letter to the *Cork Constitution* of 1 February 1888, responded to these complaints with the claim that the Trustees had 'contracted for the erection of sixteen houses at a cost of over £2,500'.[9] Mr. Freke's letter provoked a reporter from the *Eagle* to investigate the nature of the housing provided in Baltimore.[10] The reporter was very critical of 'the thrown down and ill-suited cottages' provided by the Carbery Estate for 'labourers, fisher-men and other poor creatures' and regarded them as inappropriate to the 'circumstances of the village and the fishing industry'. 'Seven persons . . . huddled together' in 'an old loft' were described in sardonic terms as typical 'victims of the *improvement* scheme'. Consequently, the *Eagle* promised to keep its legendary 'eye on the trustees of the Carbery Estates'.[11]

The 1891 Census recorded an increase of seventeen (from thirty-five to fifty-two) since 1881 in the number of inhabited houses in Baltimore town while the population grew from 146 people to 306 people.[12] Conversely, a decline in the number of inhabited houses from twenty-nine to twenty-four in the townland of Baltimore mirrored a population decrease from 173 people to 113 people.[13] However, the following extract from a report in the *Eagle* 15 November 1893 suggests, despite its euphoric tone, that the housing problems in Baltimore, which had evoked such criticism in the newspaper's columns in 1888, had been solved:

> thriving shops and neat dwelling houses have supplanted the former tiny incommodious cabins while almost at the foot of the very castle itself stands the terminus of the C.B. & S.C. Railway, with not very far off the sheds where the schoolboys may be seen during the fishing season, busy as bees and just as happy, hard at work curing and packing the mackerel landed at the slip by the good boat *Baroness*.[14]

The physical renewal and expansion of Baltimore is confirmed by one Henry Stanley Newman who arrived in Baltimore on 17 April 1895.[15]

By 1901 almost 92 per cent of all occupied houses in Baltimore town were categorised as class two or even better.[16] This was in stark contrast with the thirty-seven houses of the 175 inhabitants of Toe Head, where despite being a coastal community 'on a long and narrow promontory' five miles east of Baltimore, the mackerel industry had not developed.[17] Seventeen of these houses, amounting to 46 per cent of the total, were declared in 1907 by a Dr. T. J. O'Meara as 'unfit for human habitation, and of the remaining 20, all, with one or two exceptions, are defective by reason of earthen floors or insufficient ventilation'.[18] The improve-ment in housing standards in Baltimore town paralleled the infrastructural and institutional developments directly associated with Baltimore's emergence as a centre for an expanding mackerel industry in 1879.

Population increase brought not only physical changes to Baltimore town, but also a shift in the nature of the community. This was generated by the incursion into the local and long established community framework of new communities of interest associated with the mackerel industry. These included the seasonal influx of fishermen and fish buyers, those who were employed both in the fresh or in the cured mackerel industry, the crews of the visiting Norwegian ice vessels, specialists in the marine trades such as sail-making, net-making, or boatbuilding and the staff and students of the Baltimore Fishery School.

An analysis of the census returns for Baltimore town reveals that the community was not one homogenous entity. Thus on the night of the 3 April 1881 the 1881 census records that the residential community of 146 persons occupying thirty-five houses in the town, was dwarfed numerically by what may be termed a floating community of 471 persons on board sixty-one vessels, fifty-seven of which were fishing craft. The mackerel fleet was dominated by non-local fishermen whose interest in Baltimore related to its suitability as a landing place for spring mackerel from March to June and to a lesser extent for autumn mackerel. It was claimed, for instance, in 1890 that over £12,000 per week was sometimes paid for fish landed in Baltimore but that most of this money found 'its way into the houses of people living in Howth, Arklow, County Down, Isle of Man, Yarmouth and the Scotch fishery stations'.[19] Thomas Quilliam, skipper of a forty-five foot fishing boat from Peel in the Isle of Man, observed, while fishing off the south and west since 1880, the low level of involvement by the Irish fishermen.[20] He questioned how Manx fishermen like himself could 'carry our money home to the Isle of Man, and why should not they have it. It is there on their coasts, and yet we can go to their coasts and take it home from them'.[21] Mr Quilliam did not realise that he and his fellow Manx fishermen were replicating a centuries old pattern of fishermen of different nationalities fishing on a seasonal basis off Baltimore and other Atlantic coastal areas of Ireland.

Baltimore's rapid rise in reputation in the 1880s as a centre of the mackerel industry, second only to Kinsale, and its unique position between the well-established but declining Kinsale mackerel industry to the east and the under-developed mackerel industry to the west attracted comments such as: 'If anyone wants to know what can be done for the western and south-western parts of Ireland, go visit Baltimore'.[22] The focus on the name 'Baltimore' tended to obscure the fact that it was the fishermen of Cape Clear, and not those from Baltimore town or townland who pioneered and dominated local participation in the lucrative mackerel fishing. Thomas Quilliam, the fishing skipper from the Isle of Man, singled out the Cape Clear men in 1887 for their ability to compete with their English counterparts.[23] While referring to 'the fishermen from Baltimore', he added that 'The boats hail from Baltimore, but they are principally Cape Clear men in them'.[24] Similarly, the buying and marketing of the mackerel for export was largely controlled by outside interests, particularly from England but also from Scotland and America who located in Baltimore on a seasonal basis. The Baltimore Fishery Company itself had originally been founded in Baltimore in 1876 by Cornish men, with a Mr. John Cox of Cadgwith,

Cornwall, as manager, to process pilchards.[25] When it went into liquidation after three years, it was purchased by Skibbereen men, Messrs. Richard Beamish, John F. Levis and Richard Carey who competed successfully but on a smaller scale with the larger non-native companies.[26] The market control of the mackerel industry by outside interests produced artificial price cutting, even as late as 1907,[27] when the industry was in decline. This dependency on outsiders was also at variance with the self-reliance promoted by Baroness Burdett-Coutts and Fr Davis among the fishermen.

While the economic benefits of the mackerel industry were shared unequally by the various local and outside interests, the establishment of the Baltimore Fishery School in 1887 can be seen as an attempt to ensure that the new fishing skills and commercial mentality demonstrated by the fishermen of the Baltimore area would be disseminated throughout the coastal communities of Ireland as a whole but particularly along the western seaboard. However, the reluctance of fishing communities to send their sons to the school was only one of the difficulties which the trustees of the school experienced in fulfilling the original aims of its founders.[28] The restrictive nature of the Industrial Schools Act on the development of the school as a fishery school also tended to socially isolate the institution from the society of the local people. Thus the 'Orders, Rules and Regulations' relating to the daily routine, which began with the sound of a bugle at 6 a.m., indicate a rigid regime whereby 'the strictest discipline' was enforced.[29] The boys were required to write home 'at a stated time'. All mail was vetted by the superintendent and only one boy was allowed visit the post office with the bag of letters.[30] Inspector Blennerhassett[31] concluded in 1897 that this rigid enforcement of the Industrial Schools Act was incompatible with the requirements of a fishery school.[32] Sadly, his accompanying proposal, that the Baltimore National School should be closed and that the children of the parish and the boys of the Fishery School should participate together at the school in an educational programme appropriate to the needs of a fishing community, does not seem to have been implemented.[33] Thus an opportunity was missed to consolidate Baltimore's reputation as a fishing centre by providing its young people with a complementary maritime based education. A shared education would also have facilitated the integration of the Fishery School into the social fabric of the local community. There is some evidence that the active participation of the School in a variety of training and commercial skills relating to the fishing industry sometimes provoked ill-feeling rather than goodwill in the local community. Sir Thomas Brady, a member of the governing body, admitted, for instance, in response to an unfavourable report of 18 November 1896 by Inspector Blennerhassett, that the Fishery School was criticised by locals for undermining their employment prospects by involving the boys of the school in the making of fish boxes and the curing of fish.[34]

However, the Fishery School did revive traditional marine skills which bene-fited the local community as a whole. This sometimes required the importation

13. Boys of Baltimore Fishery School c. 1890s (Lawrence Collection)

of outside expertise, as in the case of sail-making and mending which employed 'one of the best and most skilled instructors from County Down' in 1896.[35] The extension of the railway to Baltimore was attributed in 1890 to the 'widespread publicity' which was accorded to 'Baltimore as a successful fishing station' with the founding of the Fishery School in 1887.[36] Fr Davis, in particular, skilfully promoted the new Fishery School as an international icon of Baltimore's maritime identity. The official inquiry regarding the proposed railway was held at the Fishery School in January 1890, and Fr Davis in his evidence referred to 'communications from the Danish and Belgian Consuls about that school with a view to establishing ones in their kingdoms'.[37] The Fishery School was regarded as a showpiece for visiting dignitaries.

The international character (a feature of the spring rather than of the autumn fishery) of the mackerel fleet can be illustrated by referring to the annual report of the Inspectors of Irish Fisheries for 1890 which shows that on one day a fleet of 119 boats fishing off Baltimore consisted of sixty Irish, thirty Manx, twenty-five English and four French.[38] Essentially nomadic by nature, this transient community was defined by the variable habits of migratory mackerel and fluctuating market prices rather than the community values of Baltimore.

Nevertheless, even if these nautical nomads were the prime beneficiaries of Baltimore's natural advantages as a landing and distribution centre for mackerel, in return they drew the native communities of Baltimore and the surrounding district into a wider world of a maritime economy based on cash, entrepreneurial

skills and new fishing technology. This new mind set was complemented by an
awakening of Baltimore's maritime identity and vitality as a seaport. This is
reflected in the following extract from a poem about the 1896 fishing season
by John O'Reilly, a schoolteacher from Sherkin Island:[39]

> On Saturday night there is far greater racket,
> On Baltimore square than on Billingsgate Market
> With fiddlers and packmen, street singers and showmen,
> Fat Frenchmen, fair Manx men and numbers of Norsemen.

The cosmopolitan atmosphere in the above lines is expressed in more prosaic
terms in the annual report of the Inspectors of Irish Fisheries for 1896.[40] This
does not refer to the crews of the Norwegian ice vessels but it shows that the
spring mackerel fleet of ninety-five vessels,[41] though on the decline and
increasingly dominated by Irish boats, consisted of seventy Irish, fifteen Manx,
five English, two Scotch and three French. In demographic terms this added
up to over 700 men, as each vessel could have had a crew of eight men. The
social vacuum which occurred in the aftermath of the Spring season is evident
from the following description,

> Matters are now very quiet in Baltimore; all the fishing boats have left
> the harbour, and in consequence an air of languid inactivity prevails all
> around. The place is at once transformed from a busy bustling seaport
> into a veritable deserted village.[42]

Public houses provided a welcome respite for fishermen who were paid on
Saturdays as it was 'usual that fishermen are utterly parched with the thirst after
the week's fishing'.[43] Information on the extent of this thirst and the nature
of the drinking ambience is sparse but John Ferguson, a fisherman from
Kilkeel, County Down, revealed at Skibbereen Petty Sessions that himself,
John McKee and three other fishermen had consumed 'two and a half gallons
of porter' between them from nine o'clock to half past ten, while ashore at
Baltimore on 29 April 1893.[44] Unfortunately, this social interlude concluded
with a serious assault on Ferguson by a local individual named Andrew
Crowley. Crowley's contention that he had been provoked by the insulting
remarks of the northern men who shouted: 'To hell with Home Rule' and
challenged 'any b——y Irishman to fight him' did not earn him any sympathy
with the magistrates, as he was sentenced to fourteen days with hard labour.[45]
Another Kilkeel fisherman, William McKnight who had also been assaulted
by Crowley, stated that he had been fishing in Baltimore for sixteen or
seventeen years and had never seen anything like it before.

One can assume that the eight vintners listed for Baltimore in 1895 enjoyed
considerable customer loyalty among the fishing community both native and
nomadic.[46] However, the 'floating grog shops', of Dutch or French origin and

operating outside the three mile limit, provided competition in illicit goods such as brandy and tobacco.[47] These continental interlopers, while respectful of the lives and property of the fishermen, were perceived to pose a moral threat. The Fisheries Committee of the Royal Dublin Society was adamant that 'this unmitigated curse should not be allowed to gain foothold in our fisheries'.[48] One such vessel, appropriately called *Cosmopolitan*, was eventually arrested when it strayed inside the three mile limit near Baltimore.[49] Conchúr Ó Síocháin and his fellow crew members from Cape Clear suffered a similar fate in 1895 when they returned to Baltimore with brandy and tobacco concealed under the mackerel nets. They had bought the contraband from a Dutch smuggler, known as *Lord John*.[50]

An interesting example of social integration is revealed eight years later in the 1901 census household returns.[51] A Dennis Sweeney described himself as head of a family consisting of his wife, Mary, and his twenty-six year old son, Michael who was a fisherman. However, the household also included another fisherman named John Polon, his wife Mary and their two children. The Polon family were defined as lodgers and whereas John Polon was born in County Down, his wife, their two children and the Sweeney family were born in County Cork. Similarly, the lack of sailmaking facilities which Fr Davis lamented in 1886[52] must have attracted sailmaker William Logan to Baltimore as he stated in the 1901 census household return that though his wife, Margaret, himself and three of his children were born in County Antrim, another child was born in County Wicklow and the three younger children were born in County Cork. Even in 1920, he was still listed as the only sailmaker in Baltimore.[53]

An analysis of the 1901 census household returns for the town of Baltimore reveals that, of the 125 residents with stated occupations, nineteen people (14.7 per cent) were not born in the county of Cork.[54] While thirteen of these people came from different counties in Ireland, six people referred to England, Scotland or the Isle of Man as their place of birth. Of the six coastguards, all were born in England except chief boatman, John Mahoney, who stated that he was born in Highfield, Cork. The four members of the Royal Irish Constabulary were all born in Ireland but only Constable John Joseph Caven was born in the county of Cork. Of the nineteen vessels listed in the shipping return,[55] the 350 ton brigantine, *Echo*', was the largest with a Norwegian crew of eight men and a Swedish captain named Augustinus Adamson. The crews of nine vessels, mostly engaged in fishing, were born in the county of Cork but the fishermen in the other fishing vessels came from counties Wicklow and Down with two fishing smacks registered in North Shields in Northumbria on the east coast of England. All of the thirty-five people with listed occupations in the townland of Baltimore were born in County Cork.

While the harvest of the sea fuelled Baltimore's development as a seaport from 1880, many other coastal communities with a subsistent agricultural economy experienced extreme hardship after a succession of bad harvests. Allied to this hardship was the increasing political agitation to transfer the ownership of the land from the landlords to the tenant occupiers. Thus the 'Land Question' occupied centre stage of both national and local politics. Contemporaneously, a marginalised but vocal minority highlighted the value of developing a complementary maritime economy based on Ireland's underdeveloped fisheries. Dr. John de Courcy Ireland refers in particular to 'a persistent and admirably well-informed campaign in favour of developing our fisheries' by the journal, *The Irish Builder*, during the 1870s and 1880s.[56] It gave prominent coverage to the reports of the parish priest of Baltimore and the Islands, Fr Davis, and other promoters of the fishing industry, on how 'Baltimore, a decaying village, became the centre of a great industry'.[57] Fr Davis was a skilful and persistent promoter of Baltimore as an exemplar for the development of fishing as a national industry. The international media coverage which accompanied the opening of the Baltimore Fishery School in 1887 by Baroness Burdett-Coutts reflected a highly developed media sense by Fr Davis. 'The silver tongue of Munster',[58] as Fr Davis was called, used his persuasive powers to lobby politicians and government officials at an international and national level.

The central role which Fr Davis played in the establishment of the Baltimore and Skibbereen Harbour Board in 1884 demonstrates the efficacy of his political skills at a local level. The joint title of the Baltimore and Skibbereen Harbour Board masks the intense rivalry which characterised the negotiations between the representatives of Baltimore and Skibbereen prior to the establishment of the Board. Skibbereen's situation on the tidal river Ilen, which flowed into Baltimore Harbour, provided limited access to the sea and added a maritime dimension to an otherwise land defined town. Despite navigation constraints, the Town Commissioners of Skibbereen considered it 'vitally important' for 'the commercial, sanitary and agricultural interests of Skibbereen and its neighbours', to form 'a Harbour Board for the port of Skibbereen'. A public meeting in Skibbereen to consider this proposal was reported in detail by the *Eagle* 3 March 1883. This meeting was attended by 'a goodly contingent from Baltimore' who relied almost exclusively on Fr Davis as spokesman to oppose the exclusion of the name Baltimore from the title of the Board. At this and subsequent meetings Fr Davis concentrated on portraying Baltimore's superior maritime pedigree. He ridiculed the notion of the 'Port of Skibbereen' in terms that evoked laughter at the meeting. He juxtaposed his jibe with his claim that 'for three centuries the Port of Baltimore had been known as a remarkable port'. His allusions to Baltimore's maritime heritage were skilfully linked to his emphasis on Baltimore's contemporary strategic position in the mackerel industry. While his rose-tinted view of Baltimore's maritime history went unchallenged, his claim that in 1883 it was 'a great central station of deep sea fisheries for the south-west coast of Ireland' provoked sceptical but prophetic remarks from Mr. F.P.E. Potter, Town Commissioner and owner of the *Eagle*, about the unreliable nature of the fishing industry. However, Fr Davis's passionate exposition of Baltimore's well-anchored maritime identity ensured that, despite Skibbereen's demographic and commercial superiority, the two towns would be 'twins'. Thus the meeting finally concluded with the unanimous acceptance of the amended proposal that a Skibbereen and Baltimore Harbour Board be formed.

An unexpected obstacle was the scepticism of the Trustees of the Carbery Estates who were dubious regarding the joint board's suitability for protecting 'the interests of Baltimore'. Furthermore, as 'lords of the soil', even if they were non-resident in Baltimore, they politely but firmly rejected Fr Davis' entitlement to act 'as our spokesman'. Nevertheless, when the new board was legally constituted in 1884 as the Baltimore and Skibbereen Harbour Board, not only was Baltimore to the fore but Fr Davis became its first chairman until his death in 1892.[59] The founding of the Harbour Board may be seen as the re-emergence of the 'historic little town'[60] of Baltimore from the shadow of a younger Skibbereen and the reassertion of its superior maritime pedigree.

Fr Davis' preoccupation with the development of maritime resources, did not preclude an awareness of the role of agriculture in the changing economic and political life of his parishioners. There is no doubt that the principles of land ownership articulated by the newly established Land League concurred with the measures he initiated with Baroness Burdett-Coutts to enable fishermen to own their own boats and compete successfully with foreign fishermen. Baltimore town and townland were part of the 5,000 acre Carbery estate.[61] Lord Carbery lived, however, in Castlefreke at Rosscarbery, twenty miles east of Baltimore on the coast. Thus it was Fr Davis and not the Carbery family who in the course of giving evidence to the Bessborough Commission on 4 November 1880, stated that 'I am pretty well conversant with the tenure of land in West Carbery'.[62] Fr Davis also contended that the rents on Lord Carbery's estate were 'fair', in consequence of which he was of the opinion that the tenants 'had nothing to complain about'.[63] However, he also expressed his support for the 'establishment of a peasant proprietary', albeit on a gradual basis, although he was opposed to the demise of 'the resident gentry of the country'.[64]

He reminded the Commission that many small tenant-farmers could not survive without fishing despite being ill-equipped for the task. He highlighted the paradox of Baltimore's natural resources when he contrasted the poverty of the soil with the abundance of the sea whose riches were under-exploited. While he strongly advocated the economic advantage of fostering fishing as an industry, he also added a political dimension when he suggested that it would lead to 'a happy and contented people along this coast.' In equating economic prosperity with political stability, Fr Davis demonstrated his commitment to alleviating poverty while accepting the political status quo.

It seems that Baltimore's increasing prosperity due to the mackerel industry was conducive to agrarian contentment. Conversely, in other coastal communities agrarian agitation became synonymous with increasing violence as relationships between landlords and police tenants deteriorated. In the constabulary district of Skibbereen, thirty outrages were reported in 1880 with an increase to fifty-six in 1881.[65] A riot in the town of Skull on 7 June 1881, involving an estimated 2,000 to 3,000 people, eight police and six members of the coastguard, culminated in the wrecking of the police station, the house and horse-drawn car of a man 'who had been in the habit of conveying the police by car'.[66] Baltimore coastguard personnel, while returning to Baltimore by boat from Skull, were physically threatened and verbally abused by three boatloads of men from Hare Island for having conveyed reinforcements totalling fifteen police by boat to Skull. John Halsey, officer in charge of Baltimore Coastguard Station, revealed that the islanders had threatened that they would 'come over some night and wreck the station and village of Baltimore'.[67] Though the naval authorities considered sending reinforcements to Baltimore, the threat from the islanders does not seem to have materialised. When the gunboat, *Britomart*, eventually visited Baltimore on 29 June 1881 to check the security of the newly-built station[68], the commander concluded that there was 'little fear' that it would be attacked.[69]

It is significant that there is no evidence of animosity among the people of Baltimore district itself towards the police or coastguard or solidarity with either the Hare islanders or people of Skull. It is not unreasonable to assume that the growing prosperity associated with the fledgling spring mackerel industry in Baltimore would take precedence over the politics of the Land League. As the *Britomart* steamed into Baltimore harbour, the twelve week spring mackerel season of 1881 was concluding with total landings worth £15,954 which was an increase of 59.8 per cent on the 1880 landings of £9,982. The building of the new fishery pier (South Pier) between 1880 and 1883 was providing further employment. Apart from the money earned by the fishermen, Fr Davis claimed that 126 men, employed in June 1887 packing and icing mackerel, were 'each paid 25s. a week, and those men would not have earned 5s. a week at agricultural labour'. The shopkeepers and publicans in Baltimore stood to make a substantial income from the crews of the fishing vessels. Sir Thomas Brady, Inspector of Irish Fisheries, asserted that it cost £48 11s. 6d. to provision the *Sir Edward Birkbeck* fishing vessel for the 1887 mackerel season.[70]

While the Ireland of the 1880s was consumed by the politics of agrarian agitation and legislative reform, Fr Davis addressed his considerable political skills to promoting the 'the welfare of the Irish fishermen.'[71] His belief in the value of developing fishing as a national industry, was fuelled by his admiration for the skill and speed with which the Cape Clear fishermen had mastered the technology and techniques of modern deep-sea fishing and acted as conduits of change for a new generation of fishermen in the wider Baltimore district.

However, unlike the fishermen of the east coast and those of Kinsale, Baltimore fishermen were predominantly part-time. Fr Davis accepted the part-time mentality of the fishermen as 'in Baltimore all our men have a little patch of ground, and in winter they are engaged in preparing it . . . for the production of potatoes and a little milk and a little butter'.[72] The new mackerel industry with a short season (from March to June) was well suited to this dual economy as it was traditionally believed 'that the man who had not planted his potatoes by the first fortnight in March would be in a bad way'.[73]

The contrast between the co-existence of imported modern fishing technology with subsistence agricultural practices centred on the spade is accentuated by the claim of Fr Davis that 'in Baltimore it is the men who work the boats that are the owners of the boats . . . they are like "peasant-proprietors on the ocean"'.[74] He contrasted them with their counterparts in 'Skibbereen and other places, where shopkeepers provide the boats.'

A campaign for the establishment of the Baltimore Fishery School was initiated by the Catholic bishop of Ross, Dr. Fitzgerald in 1885 and consisted of lobbying government officials through letters and delegations. The success of the 'peasant-proprietors on the ocean' in Baltimore proved to be of central importance in gaining government approval in the autumn of 1885.[75] Later in the spring of 1887 the Trustees of the school, in the course of a submission to the new chief secretary in Ireland, Arthur Balfour, for a parliamentary grant of £10,000, described the Baltimore fishermen as follows:

> . . . absorbed in their remunerative work they have kept themselves free from political agitation . . . this part of Ireland, although situated in one of the most disturbed counties, having remained entirely peaceful and quiet during the late troubles . . . we submit this as a striking instance of the political value of encouragements given to trade and commerce . . .[76]

Subsequently, a politically charged sermon by one of the founders and trustees of the school, Dr. Fitzgerald, was reported by the *Eagle* on 21 January 1888 under the heading of 'The bishop of Ross on Coercion'. The report referred in particular to his criticism of 'our present rulers' for resorting to repressive legislation which contravened people's right 'to live in befitting comfort and independence in the land that gave them birth'.

The humanitarian concerns which underpinned Dr. Fitzgerald's sermon were shared in equal measure with Fr Davis, even if the bishop tended to be more overtly political. Fr Davis's preoccupation with piscatorial politics involved him in behind the scenes 'appeals in high quarters' and the collaboration of his 'many influential friends'.[77] This approach was at variance with the confrontational tactics and the mass mobilisation of public support associated with Land League politics. Nevertheless, the lobbying techniques of Fr Davis were singled out as being instrumental in promoting Baltimore's piscatorial based prosperity which put his parishioners 'beyond the fear of want' while the failure of the potato harvest in the wet summer of 1890 brought widespread distress among the agrarian based economies along the south and west coast.[78] The vulnerability of a potato-dependent economy, highlighted by the 1890 distress, was one of the chief factors which persuaded Balfour to establish the Congested Districts Board in 1891 as part of the Land Act of 1891. While Baltimore was included as a congested district and Fr Davis was appointed to the Board, ironically its status as a successful mackerel fishery centre ensured that the Congested Districts Board resources were largely devoted to the west coast communities where the mackerel industry was almost non-existent. By 1892 the Congested Districts Board had established on the west coast a spring mackerel fishery[79] whose growth would be a further influential factor in Baltimore's declining mackerel industry.

Apart from the external factors which hastened the decline of the mackerel industry in Baltimore, nobody of the calibre of the late Fr Davis emerged from the community to facilitate the necessary changes at a local level. This is exemplified by the ineffectual efforts of the Harbour Board to ensure the construction of a new fishing pier and its connection to the new railway line. At a Board meeting 12 August 1893 Sir Thomas Brady and the other members endeavoured to persuade Lord Carbery 'to ratify the action of the Harbour Board by giving us your powerful influence, as lord of the soil, for the realisation of this most important and indispensable work'.[80] Lord Carbery's lukewarm support for the project and his lack of commitment to developing the fishing industry is evident from his contention that 'they had got a good deal there in Baltimore already'.

The lord of the soil seemed indifferent to the plight of his tenants who were curing fish in unsuitable conditions, even though he was reminded by a Mr. Sheehy that it 'would pay him well' to build a proper facility. His promise 'to note and remember' the concerns of the harbour commissioners is hardly reinforced by the parting remark attributed to him 'that he regretted that the place was so inconvenient from Rosscarbery for him to visit more frequently'. It is no surprise that over a year later the *Eagle* reported that the fish-curing industry at Baltimore still suffered from inadequate curing facilities due to the failure of Lord Carbery to fulfil his promises.[81]

As the mackerel industry continued to decline, a significant event during this period was the decision of the Trustees of the Carbery Estates on November 1904 to instruct their agents, J.B. Stewart and Sons, to commence negotiations for the sale of their estates to their tenants under the Irish Land Act of 1903.[82] Purchase agreements were concluded with the twenty-two tenants of the Carbery Estates in Baltimore townland by 30 April 1908, whereas most of the town of Baltimore was excluded from the sale.[83]

In the 1901 census for the townland of Baltimore, out of forty-five listed occupations, the largest single occupational category consisted of ten farmers as opposed to nine fishermen but in view of the seasonal nature of fishing it is quite likely that individuals would engage in a dual economy. In the town of

Baltimore, where 125 occupations are listed, the same ambiguity arises regarding the seven men in the labouring category. Twelve individuals fall within a farming designation. However, apart from six individuals who are termed 'farmer' and Daniel Mahony who, as head of the household, described himself as 'farmer and fisherman', there were other farming variations as for instance, in the case of Cornelius Hegarty, who described himself as a 'farmer and publican'. However, 'fisherman' constituted the largest single category with sixteen men enumerated. A further analysis of the occupational structure of the household returns for Baltimore town reveals sixteen other maritime occupations, though not all were necessarily directly related to the fishing industry.

While the evidence of this research points to the dominance of outsiders in the mackerel industry in Baltimore, nevertheless it is surprising that Patrick Cottrell was the only head of household who described himself as a 'fish buyer'. Thus Thomas Salter, who defined himself as a 'publican' in the 1901 census form, described himself in 1907 as a 'curer . . . for several years' to the chief inspector of Irish fisheries, Rev. W.S. Green.[84] Despite the limitations of the census form, especially when householders were engaged in more than one occupation, the information extracted from it does demonstrate the development of marine occupations such as sailmaking and boatbuilding which had been absent in 1886.

Apart from the specific onshore marine services which the mackerel industry encouraged, the 1901 census reveals a variety of general commercial services such as grocer shops, lodging houses and a total of seven public houses whose trade linked directly to the mackerel industry. The extension of the railway to Baltimore in 1893, primarily to transport mackerel, created an 'influx of strangers . . . [who] settled down for some weeks' in Baltimore, although it was suggested that some visitors 'were leaving owing to the disagreeable odours arising from the cleansing of the fish on the piers, so near their lodgings'.[85] However, the visitors continued to come to Baltimore and in 1907 it was claimed 'that a lot of people take houses there in the summer time. It is a very nice seaside place'.[86] The advent of the railway also provided employment in Baltimore. This is reflected in the 1901 census which enumerated six men, including the station master, Rowland Campion, who were railway employees. The six married coastguard officers recorded in the census, apart from the general maritime nature of their work, monitored the movements of the fishing fleet and provided statistics on boats and fish landings.[87]

Conclusion

'It has been well observed that that the Irish fisheries seemed to exist for the benefit of people of all countries save and except the Irish themselves'.[1] This statement by Fr. Davis encapsulates the historical context within which the people of Baltimore and the surrounding district benefited from the spring and autumn mackerel fisheries between 1879 and 1913 has been investigated. The emergence of Baltimore from 1879 as a leading centre of the mackerel industry, largely dominated by outsiders, was shown to be the product of human and natural factors peculiar to that time. The failure of the people of Baltimore to capitalise on their fishing resources, in contrast with the success of visiting fishermen from England and continental Europe, exemplified the backward state of fishing among the coastal communities, apart from Kinsale, along the south and west coast. The fishing trade, particularly since the Famine, suffered severely from a shortage of capital, inefficient fishing practices, inadequate market opportunities and a lack of leadership and entrepreneurial endeavour. However, the arrival in 1879 of Fr. Davis in Baltimore as parish priest and his collaboration with another outsider, the philanthropic Baroness Burdett-Coutts, provided the leadership that enabled Baltimore to capitalise on the new opportunities afforded by fortuitous changes in the mackerel industry. Equally fortuitous was the active involvement of the enlightened inspector of fisheries, Sir Thomas Brady, who pioneered the concept of the Baltimore Fishery School and, even at the age of seventy-two years in 1896, laboured to prevent the closure of the school. Other influential supporters of Fr. Davis and active proponents of Baltimore's maritime development as an exemplar for the nation included his clerical superior, Bishop Fitzgerald, and fishery inspector, Rev. W.S. Green. When Fr. Davis died in 1892, as landings of mackerel were declining, nobody with his charismatic personality or maritime vision emerged from within or outside the local community to replace him.

Fr. Davis's determination to develop a locally based fishing industry was fuelled by his knowledge of the poverty of many of his parishioners despite their proximity to rich fishing grounds. The low level of local enterprise in the development of both maritime and agrarian resources in Baltimore was a microcosm of Ireland itself. Thus, Baltimore's importance as a landing place for mackerel was primarily dependent on non-local fishermen with superior catching power and English fish buyers who dominated the marketing and distribution of the mackerel. The English fish buyers provided the capital, structures and organisation which, apart from that supplied by the Baltimore

Fishery Company, were non-existent in Baltimore for marketing the increasing volume of mackerel landings in Baltimore from 1880 onwards. The preparation of fresh mackerel for export to England and cured mackerel for export to America made Baltimore a centre of extensive and remunerative onshore employment that brought economic prosperity. However, a statistical analysis of the mackerel landings in Baltimore over thirty-one years reveals the volatile nature of the mackerel industry. The short term nature of Baltimore's economic success as a landing place for mackerel may be attributed to insufficient local control over the catching and marketing of the fish and a failure to develop a market within Ireland. Nevertheless, the mackerel industry did underpin the development of Baltimore's marine infrastructure, the Baltimore Fishery School and the Baltimore Extension Railway.

The visiting fishermen served as role models for local fishermen. It was Cape Clear fishermen, however, rather than fishermen from Baltimore itself, who were the first to invest in the superior boats and equipment of the outsiders with the assistance of the Burdett-Coutts fund. This initiative formed the nucleus of an expanding local deep sea fleet. However, the locally based fleet never expanded sufficiently to maintain the level of mackerel landings of the 1880s. The number of visiting fishermen using Baltimore as their base declined from the 1890s onwards. The aspirations of the founders of the Baltimore Fishery School in 1887 to provide modern training on board its own fishing boats for young people from the fishing communities on a national basis achieved limited success due, in particular, to the restrictions of the Industrial Schools Act. However, the Fishery School did become a centre for maritime enterprise where traditional skills, such as netmaking and fishcuring, were revived and taught in a commercial context. The opening of a boatyard in the school, not only drew on boatbuilding skills traditional to Baltimore, but also introduced new designs along the lines of the fishing boats built in the Isle of Man. The achievements of the Baltimore Fishery School during the period of this study may not have matched the aspirations of its enlightened and idealistic founders. Nevertheless, it represented an enlightened attempt at combining education with maritime enterprise. The closure of the school in 1950 and the subsequent legal proceedings surrounding the derelict property have obscured its former national status as an icon of a developing native Irish fishing industry. Baltimore is no longer a centre of the mackerel industry which had been the catalyst for physical, economic and social transformation between 1879 and 1913. The small fleet of vessels which fish for white fish or lobster during the summer and herring during the winter belie Baltimore's brief role as a model for the fishing communities of Ireland.

Notes

ABBREVIATIONS

Archive Organisations

A.P.	Admiralty Publications
B.T.	Board of Trade
C.D.B.	Congested Districts Board
C.A.I.	Cork Archives Institute
D.A.T.I.	Department of Agriculture and Technical Instruction
I.F.C.	Irish Folklore Collection, Roinn Béaloideas Éireann, University College Dublin, Main Manuscripts Collection
N.A.I.	National Archives of Ireland
N.L.I.	National Library of Ireland
N.U.I.M.	National University of Ireland, Maynooth
O.P.W.	Office of Public Works
O.S.	Ordnance Survey Ireland
P.R.O.	Public Record Office, London
R.C.B.	Library of the Representative Church Body of the Church of Ireland

Journals etc.

C.E.	*Cork Examiner*
F.J.	*Freemans's Journal*
S.S.	*Southern Star*
I.B.	*The Irish Builder*
J.C.H.A.S.	*Journal of the Cork Historical and Archaeological Society*
J.K.A.S.	*Journal of the Kerry Archaeological and Historical and Society*

Parliamentary Papers

I.R.C.	*Vice-regal commission on Irish railways, including light railways, 1907.*
R.C.C.I.	*Royal commission on congestion in Ireland.*
R.C.I.P.W.	*Royal commission on Irish public works; appendix to second report of the royal commission on Irish public works, minutes of proceedings, evidence, and index* [C. 5264–1], H.C. 1888, xlviii, 1.
R.I.I.F.	*Annual report of the inspectors of Irish fisheries on the sea and inland fisheries of Ireland.*

INTRODUCTION

1 Daniel Donovan, *Sketches in Carbery* (Cork, 1876, reprint 1979), p. 23.

2 Anon., *Baltimore industrial fishing school: extracts from opinions of the press* (Dublin, 1888), pp 51–2.

3 Rev. Charles Davis, *Deep sea fisheries of Ireland* (Dublin 1886), p. 24.

4 Riobárd P. Breatnach, *The man from Cape Clear* (Dublin and Cork, 1975), translation of Conchúr Ó Síocháin's *Seanchas Chléire* (Baile Átha Cliath, 1940).

5 Donncha Ó Cróinín, (ed.), *Seanachas ó Chairbre 1* (Baile Átha Cliath, 1985).

6 Cormac Ó Gráda, *Ireland: a new economic history 1780–1939* (Oxford, 1994), p. 148.

BALTIMORE AND THE SEA

1 *Report on the memorials presented to the lords of the admiralty with reference to the harbours and lighthouses of county Cork*, H.C. 1849 (97), xlix, 385, p. 5.

2 John de Courcy Ireland, 'Introduction' in Liam Blake, *Shoreline* (Dublin, 1991), p. 12.

3 *Sailing directions for the coast of Ireland, part 1* (Admiralty publication, 1877).

4 *Eagle*, 3 Feb. 1883; See also *Report on the harbours and lighthouses of county Cork*, p. 6.

5 Donovan, *Sketches in Carbery*, p. 20.

6 Pádraig Ó Maidín, 'Pococke's tour of south and south-west Ireland in 1758' in *J.C.H.A.S.*, lxii (1958), p. 81.

7 According to an admiralty report in 1848, the pier was built in 1828. See *Report on the harbours and lighthouses of county Cork*, p. 6.

8 Samuel Lewis, *A topographical dictionary of Ireland*, (2 vols, London, 1837), ii, p. 172.

9 Lewis, *Topographical dictionary*, i, p. 249.

10 Lewis, *Topographical dictionary*, i, p. 249.

11 Lewis, *Topographical dictionary*, i, p. 172.

12 *Appendix to the first report of the commissioners appointed to inquire into the municipal corporations in Ireland, part 1* [henceforth cited as *Inquiry 1835*], H.C. 1835 (27), xxviii, 1, p. 3(with thanks to Liam Clare for this reference).

13 *Inquiry 1835*; p. 3, Lewis, *Topographical dictionary*, i, pp 172 3.

14 *Inquiry 1835*, p. 3.

15 The title of baroness was bestowed on her by Queen Victoria in 1871. See Edna Healey, *Lady unknown- the life of Angela Burdett-Coutts* (London, 1978), p. 131.

16 Duchess of Teck, *The Baroness Burdett-Coutts* (Chicago, 1893), p. 131.

17 Teck, *Baroness Burdett-Coutts*, p. 129.

18 Davis, *Cape Clear: a retrospect*, p. 486.

19 *I.B.*, 15 Feb. 1876, p. 54.

20 *I.B.*, 15 Feb. 1876, p. 54.

21 *I.B.*, 15 Feb. 1876, p. 54.

22 *I.B.*, 15 Oct 1884, p. 311.

23 Davis, *Cape Clear: a retrospect*, p. 486.

24 Teck, *Baroness Burdett-Coutts*, p. 148.

25 Teck, *Baroness Burdett-Coutts*, p. 148.

26 *I.B.*, 15 March 1881, p. 76.

27 *Eagle and County Cork Advertiser*, (henceforth cited as *Eagle*), Sat. 15 Oct. 1892.

28 *Report of her majesty's commissioners of inquiry into the working of the landlord and tenant (Ireland) act, 1870 and the acts amending the same* [C.2779], H.C. 1881 xix,1, p. 902.

29 *Landlord and tenant (Ireland) act, 1870, inquiry*, p. 902.

30 *Eagle*, 17 March 1883.

31 *I.B.*, 15 Feb. 1876, p. 54.

32 *I.B.*, 15 Feb. 1876, p. 54.

33 Anon., *Baltimore fishing school*, p. 6.

THE ECONOMIC IMPACT OF THE BALTIMORE MACKEREL INDUSTRY

1 *Eagle* 15 October 1893.

2 *C.E.*, 15 June 1885.

3 *The Irish Crisis of 1879–80: proceedings of the Dublin Mansion House relief committee, 1880* (Dublin, 1881), pp 47–51.

4 R.V. Comerford, 'The politics of distress, 1877–82', in W.E. Vaughan (ed.), *A new history of Ireland, vi, Ireland under the Union, ii, 1870–1921* (Oxford 1996), p. 34; James S. Donnelly jr., *The land and the people of nineteenth-century Cork* (London, 1975), p. 259.

5 *Annual report of the local government board for Ireland, being the eight report under the Local Government Board (Ireland) Act, 35 & 36 Vic., c. 69* [C.2603], H.C. 1880, xxviii, 1, p. 77.

6 R.I.I.F., *1880* [C.2871], H.C. 1881, xxiii, 401, p. 40.

7 A further £800 was contributed by Lord Carbery and a total of £3,000 from the government. *Report of the joint committee of the Duchess of Malborough and Dublin Mansion House relief fund* 1881 (326), lxxv, 859, p. 13. See also *C.E.*, i, Feb. 1888.

8 *Mansion House relief committee, 1880,* p. 212.

9 *C.E.*, 22 April 1880.

10 P.R.O. File ADM 149/8. One of a fleet of eight naval vessels engaged in relief service to the maritime communities between Baltimore and Tory Island. See *Correspondence relative to measures for the relief of distress in Ireland, 1879–80,* [C.2506], H.C.1880, lxii, 187, pp 1–6.

11 P.R.O., File ADM 149/8.

12 Ibid.

13 R.C.I.P.W., p. 758; N.A.I., Crime branch special, file 9157/S, 26 October 1884.

14 R.C.I.P.W., p. 758.

15 R.I.I.F., 1882, [C.3605], H.C. 1883, xvii, 557, p. 5. Though a variety of craft were used, the Isle of Man built vessels of 30 tons or more were regarded as superior. See Colman O Mahony, 'Fishing in 19th century Kinsale' in *J.C.H.A.S.*, xcviii (1993), pp 115–6.

16 R.I.I.F., 1882, [C.3605], H.C. 1883, xvii, 557, p. 5

17 R.I.I.F, *1879* [C. 2627], H.C. 1880, xiv, 533. p. 7; Report confirmed in R.I.I.F,. *1881* [C.3248], H.C. 1882, xvii, 557, p. 7.

18 R.I.I.F, *1880* [C.2871], H.C. 1881, xxiii , 401, p. 5.

19 R.I.I.F., *1881* [C.3248], H.C. 1882, xvii, 557, p. 5.

20 R.I.I.F, *1890* [C.6403], H.C. 1890–91, xxi, 299, p. 12; This increase reflects, not only the development of the mackerel industry westwards, but also improved methods of collecting accurate statistics. Deficiencies relating to fishery statistics are discussed in various reports and especially R.I.I.F., *1886*, [C.5035] H.C. 1887, xxi, 165, p. 34.

21 N.A.I., O.P.W. 38369/80.

22 R.I.I.F, *1880*, p. 5.

23 *Eagle*, 3 Mar. 1883.

24 R.I.I.F., *1881*, p. 7.

25 Green, 'Fisheries of North America', p. 28.

26 R.I.I.F, *1888* [C.5777], H.C. 1889, xxii, 313, p. 12.

27 *I.B.*, 15 March 1881, p. 76.

28 Appointed as an Inspector of Fisheries in 1890. A profile of his life (1847–1919) by Arthur A.J. Went, 'William Spotswood Green' in *The Proceedings of the Royal Dublin Society*, series B, vol. 2, no. 3 (1967).

29 Rev. W.S. Green, 'Second report on the sea fisheries of the south and south-west coast of Ireland in Proceedings of the Royal Dublin Society, cxxiv (1888), p. 7.

30 R.I.I.F, *1883* [C.4109], H.C. 1884, xviii, 505, p. 4.

31 Fr Davis complained that it was easier to find fresh fish in the manufacturing towns of England than in the interior of Ireland. See Davis, *Fisheries of Ireland*, p. 25; *D.A.T.I., Journal no. 1* (1900), p. 195.

32 *Eagle*, 17 March 1883.

33 R.I.I.F, *1881*, p. 6.

34 Marc Bloch, *The historian's craft* (Manchester, 1997) p. 160.

35 *Eagle,* 17 March 1883.

36 Séamus Mac Gearailt, 'Mackerel and the making of Baltimore co. Cork 1879–1913', M.A. thesis 1998, N.U.I.M., pp 35–55.

37 Traditionally, the fishermen sold the mackerel to the buyers by number rather than by weight. The fish was counted by the 'hundred' which in reality totalled 126 fish consisting of 42 'casts, of three fish each and six

extra fish for the buyer. See Marion
Gunn, *Céad fáilte go Cléire* (Naas,
1990), pp 151–3

38 *R.I.I.F., 1890* [C.6403], H.C.
    1890–91, xxi, 299, p. 12.
39 Ibid., pp 17–9.
40 Ibid., p. 12.
41 A similar observation in Vivienne
    Pollock's, 'The seafishing industry of
    Co. Down', D. Phil thesis,
    University of Ulster 1988, p. 549.
42 Frank Forde, *Maritime Arklow*
    (Dublin, 1988), p. 250.
43 W.J. Micks *An account of the
    constitution . . . of the Congested
    Districts Board for Ireland, 1891–1923*
    (Dublin, 1925), p. 63; I.R.C.,
    *Appendix to the third report, minutes of
    evidence and documents relating thereto*
    [Cd.4054], H.C. 1908, xlviii, 5,
    p. 311.
44 *R.I.I.F., 1908*, p. vii.
45 *D.A. T.I., Journal no. 1* (1900), p. 195.
46 *R.I.I.F., 1911* [Cd.6473], H.C.
    1912–3, xxvii, 1, p. 11.
47 *R.I.I.F., 1888*, p. 12.
48 *R.I.I.F., 1892* [C.7048], H.C.
    1893–94, xviii, 265, p. 16.
49 *Eagle*, 3 March 1883.
50 *R.I.I.F., 1894* [C.7793], H.C. 1895,
    xx, 269, p. 87.
51 *R.C.I.P.W.*, pp 283–4.
52 *Eagle*, 3 March 1883; *C.E.*, 14 Jan.
    1890.
53 N.A.I. Crime branch special, file
    9157/S, 26 October 1894.
54 Micks, *An account of the C.D.B,* p. 63.
55 *R.I.I.F., 1889* [C.6058], H.C. 1890,
    xxi, 241, p. 8.
56 Ibid.
57 *R.I.I.F., 1890* [C.6403], H.C.
    1890–91 xxi, 299, p. 13.
58 *R.I.I.F., 1890*, p. 8.
59 Green, 'Second report', pp 47–8.
60 *R.C.I.P.W.*, p. 281.
61 *R.C.I.P.W.*, p. 281; 7s 3d. to 10s. od.
    was the average weekly wage
    quoted for west Cork in 1896 in the
    returns of the district inspectors of

the Royal Irish Constabulary. See
D.A.T.I. Journal, i, (Aug. 1900),
p. 370.
62 *R.I.I.F., 1890*, p. 13.
63 Breatnach, *The man from Cape Clear*,
    p. 29; O Mahony, 'Fishing in 19th
    century Kinsale', p. 121.
64 *R.I.I.F., 1890*, p. 13.
65 *D.A. T.I. Journal*, p. 182–3.
66 *R.C.I.P.W.*, p. 282.
67 Ibid., p. 758.
68 A voyage of 16 hours. See
    R.C.I.P.W., p. 283.
69 *R.C.I.P.W.*, p. 758.
70 *R.I.I.F., 1891* [C.6682], H.C. 1892,
    xxi, 307, p. 16.
71 *R.I.I.F., 1890*, p. 13.
72 Rev. W. S., Green, 'First report of
    survey of fishing grounds, west of
    Ireland, 1890' in *Proceedings of the
    Royal Dublin Society*, 128, pp 26–66
    (Dublin, Dec. 1890), p. 49.
73 N.A.I., Crime branch special, file
    9157/S, 26 October 1884.
74 *C.E.*, 14 Jan. 1890.
75 *R.C.I.P.W.*, p. 284.
76 *R.C.I.P.W.*, p. 284
77 *R.C.I.P.W.*, pp 282–3.
78 *R.I.I.I.F.*, *1911* [Cd.6473], H.C.
    1912–3, xxvii, 1, p. 11.
79 Green, 'Second report', p. 14.
80 *R.I.I.F., 1887* [C.5388], H.C. 1888,
    xxviii, 237, pp 7–15.
81 The Small Company, originating in
    Cornwall, set up a pilchard curing
    station in Baltimore in 1877 but it
    closed in 1879. See *R.I.I.F., 1879*
    [C.2627], H.C.1880, xiv, 533, p. 6.
82 *R.I.I.F., 1887*, p. 10
83 *R.I.I.F., 1887*, p. 7; *R.C.I.P.W.*,
    p. 739.
84 Green, 'Second report', p. 15.
85 *R.C.C.I; Appendix to the first report,
    minutes of evidence taken in Dublin, 7
    September–5 October 1906, memoranda
    and statistical tables* [Cd.3267], H.C.
    1906, vi, 389, p. 195.
86 *D.A.T.I. Journal, ii*, (Sept. 1901–June
    1902), p. 84.; *R.I.I.F., 1888*, p. 12

87 *D.A.T.I. Journal, ii,* (Sept. 1901–June 1902), p. 82.

88 *D.A.T.I. Journal, i,* (Aug. 1900), p. 686.

89 *R.I.I.F., 1888,* p. 12

90 Ibid.

91 *R.I.I.F., 1889,* p. 8

92 *R.I.I.F, 1890,* p. 20.

93 *R.C.C.I., Appendix to the first report, minutes of evidence taken in Dublin, 7 September–5 October 1906, memoranda and statistical tables* [Cd.3267], *H.C. 1906, vi, 389.,* p. 197.

94 D.A.T.I, *Report of the chief inspector of fisheries on the question of a government brand for fish cured in Ireland for export, with reports of proceedings at public meetings* (Dublin, 1907), p. 79; *Eagle,* 12 Sept. 1896.

95 D.A.T.I., *Report of fish cured,* p. 70.

96 Ibid., p. 81; *Eagle,* 11 April 1896.

97 *R.C.C.I., Appendix to the first report,* p. 197.

98 *R.I.I.F.,* 1890, p. 17.

99 *R.I.I.F,* 1890, p. 17.

100 *D.A.T.I. Journal, i* (Oct. 1911), pp 518–9; *D.A.T.I., First annual general report of the department (1900–01),* p. 207.

101 R.C.C.I., *Appendix to the first report,* p. 197

102 *D.A.T.I. Journal, i* (Oct. 1911), pp 518–27; Breatnach, *The man from Cape Clear,* p. 32.

103 Breatnach, *The man from Cape Clear,* p. 32.

104 *R.I.I.F, 1893,* pp 60–1; *R.I.I.F., 1896,* pp 96–7.

105 F.S.L., Lyons, *Ireland since the famine* (London, 1973), p. 56.

BALTIMORE'S MARITIME RENAISSANCE

1 Davis, *Deep sea fisheries,* p. 25.

2 Davis, *Deep sea fisheries,* p. 25.

3 Davis, *Deep sea fisheries,* p. 25.

4 Davis, *Deep sea fisheries,* p. 27.

5 Lewis, *A topographical dictionary of Ireland,* vol. 1, p. 172.

6 *R.I.I.F., 1879* [C.2627], H.C.1880, xiv, 533, p. 9.

7 N.A.I., OPW 38369/80; N.A.I., B.T., black, Co. Cork, file 2625.

8 Ibid.

9 Davis, 'Cape Clear: a retrospect' p. 487.

10 Davis, *Deep sea fisheries,* p. 27.

11 N.A.I., OPW 38369/80.

12 Breatnach, *The man from Cape Clear,* pp 25–33; *R.C.I.P.W.,* pp 610–1; Michael McCaughan, 'Dandys, luggers, herring and mackerel' in John Appleby and Michael McCaughan (eds), *The Irish sea* (Belfast, 1989), pp 122–3.

13 *Report of Malborough and Mansion House relief fund,* p. 2.

14 N.A.I., B.T., black, co. Cork, file 2625.

15 Breatnach, *The man from Cape Clear,* pp 25–33; *R.C.I.P.W.,* pp 610–1; McCaughan, 'Dandys, luggers, herring and mackerel', pp 122–3.

16 *R.I.I.F., 1881,* p. 4.

17 *C.E.,* 14 Jan. 1890.

18 N.A.I., B.T., green- Co. Cork, files 3666.1/2; N.A.I., B.T., black- Co. Cork, file 3240.

19 *Eagle,* 3 Feb.1893.

20 *Eagle,* 17 March 1883.

21 *The Baltimore and Skibbereen Harbour Order,* 1884 (259), iv, 435, p. 6; Government publications, *Report of the ports and harbour tribunal, 1930* (Dublin, 1930), pp 39–46;

22 Anon., *Baltimore fishing school,* p. 3.

23 D.E., Sp. Ed. File 9(a).

24 D.E., Sp. Ed. File 9(a).

25 D.E., Sp. Ed. File 9(a).

26 Anon., *Baltimore fishing school,* p. 5.

27 Anon., *Baltimore fishing school,* p. 5

28 *R.C.I.P.W.,* p. 288.

29 D.E., Sp. Ed. File 9(b); Jane Barnes, *Irish Industrial Schools 1868–1908* (Dublin, 1989), p. 128.

30 Anon., *Baltimore fishing school,* pp 144–6.

31 Archival material relating to Baltimore Fishery School in the possession of Rev. T. O'Donovan.

32 O'Donovan Archive; The lease was from 1 May 1886 under an indenture of lease dated 23 June 1886.

33 O.S., Co. Cork, 150/9, sheet 1:12500; D.E., Sp. Ed. File 9(a).

34 A total of £3,985 8s. 9d. was subscribed by 30 Oct. 1889. See archival material relating to Baltimore Fishery School in the possession of Rev. T. O'Donovan.

35 *R.C.I.P.W.*, p. 287.

36 D.E., Sp. Ed. File 9(b).

37 D.E., Sp. Ed. File 9(b).

38 Rev. Timothy O'Donovan, *The statues are rocking* (Privately published, 1987), p. 8.

39 Anon., *Baltimore fishing school*, p. 139.

40 *Eagle*, 20 Aug., 1887.

41 Anon., *Baltimore fishing school*; This book is a compilation of the reports.

42 Anon., *Baltimore fishing school*, p. 119.

43 D.E., Sp. Ed. File 9(b).

44 *R.C.I.P.W.*, p. 288.

45 *R.C.I.P.W.*, p. 603.

46 *R.C.I.P.W.*, p. 603.

47 D.E., Sp. Ed. File 9(a).

48 D.E., Sp. Ed. File 9(b).

49 O'Donovan Archive.

50 Anon., *Baltimore fishing school*, p. 72; *R.I.I.F.*, *1887*, p. 5.

51 Charles Davis, 'Cape Clear: a retrospect' in *The Month* (Sept.–Dec. 1881), p. 487.

52 *R.C.I.P.W.*, pp 287–8.

53 *R.I.I.F.*, *1890*, p. 27.

54 Breatnach, *The man from Cape Clear*, p. 29. See also Gunn, *Céad fáilte go Cléire*, p. 130.

55 The fishing boat, *Florence* from Kilkeel Co. Down, sank at the entrance to Baltimore harbour with the loss of nine fishermen during a gale on 25 April 1894. See *R.I.I.F.*, *1894* [C.7793], H.C. 1895, xx, 269, p. 6.

56 *Thirty second report I.R.I.S.*, *1893*, p. 11; A fishery school vessel, the *Sir*

Edward Birkbeck, was sunk without loss of life, after being captured by a submarine 3 May 1917: See Patrick Stevens, *British Vessels Lost at Sea 1914–18 and 1939–45* (Northamptonshire, 1988), p. 118.

57 *R.I.I.F.*, *1890*, p. 27; Henry Stanley Newman, *The harvest of the sea for Ireland* (Leominister, 1896), p. 10; *Thirty second report I.R.I.S.*, *1893*, p. 11; *Eagle*, 17 June 1893.

58 Newman, *The harvest of the sea*, p. 7.

59 D.E., Sp. Ed. File 9(a). This boat had been presented to the fishery school through the generosity of Sir Thomas Brady and a charitable fund.

60 *R.C.I.P.W.*, p. 629; *Thirty third report I.R.I.S.*, *1894*, p. 11.

61 *Thirty second report I.R.I.S.*, *1893*, p. 12.

62 O'Donovan *The statues are rocking*, p. 8.

63 *Eagle*, 7 Oct. 1896.

64 *Fiftieth report I.R.I.S.*, *1911*, p. 36.

65 *Thirty third report I.R.I.S.*, *1894*, p. 14.

66 *Thirty third report I.R.I.S.*, *1894*, p. 14; D.E., Sp. Ed. File 9(a).

67 *R.C.I.P.W.*, p. 288.

68 *R.I.I.F.*, *1889*, p. 10.

69 *R.C.I.P.W.*, p. 288.

70 *R.C.I.P.W.*, p. 288.

71 *R.I.I.F.*, *1888*, p. 12. Further curing facilities were established by English and Scotch fish buyers. See *R.I.I.F.*, *1889*, p. 8, *Eagle*, 29 Oct. 1892.

72 *R.C.I.P.W.*, p. 289.

73 *R.I.I.F.*, *1890*, pp 19–20.

74 Newman, *The harvest of the Sea*, p. 8.

75 D.E., Sp. Ed. File 9(a).

76 D.E., Sp. Ed. File 9(a); It seems netmaking eventually became a commercial success 'with a ready market' for herring and mackerel nets among the fishermen of Galway and Donegal. See D.L. Morrell, 'Life in an Irish Fisheries School' in *The Irish School Weekly* (21 Aug. 1927).

77 D.E., Sp. Ed. File 9(a). Inspector Fagan does not seem to have realised

how much the fishery school had contributed to the revival of the skills of commercial fish curing.

78 O'Donovan, *The statues are rocking*, p. 8.

79 D.E., Sp. Ed. File 9(a).

80 D.E., Sp. Ed. File 9(b).

81 D.E., Sp. Ed. File 9(a).

82 D.E., Sp. Ed. File 9(b).

83 C.A.I., Paddy O'Keefe Papers, U 180, box 10, no. 7.

84 *R.I.I.F.,1889*, p. 24; *Thirty second report I.R.I.S.*, *1893*, p. 10.

85 O'Donovan, *The statues are rocking*, p. 8.

86 O'Donovan, *The statues are rocking*, p. 8.

87 N.A.I., file no. B.V. 21, Dept. of the Marine; Micks, *An account of the C.D.B.*, pp 96–7.

88 O'Donovan, *The statues are rocking*, p. 8.

89 N.A.I., file no. B.V. 21, Dept. of the Marine.

90 A sail-powered fishing boat of Manx origin which was still functioning in 1985. For a description of this type of boat and a similar class (but of Scottish origin) known as 'zulu', see Richard C. Scott, *The Galway Hookers* (Dublin, reprint 1985) pp 77–81.

91 C.D.B., *Fisheries committee minutes*, 14 Dec. 1904.

92 *Fiftieth report I.R.I.S.*, *1911*, p. 36.

93 The *Census of Ireland, 1901* return for the Baltimore Fishery School includes a 'Thos, Moynihan, aged 14 years from Co. Cork'. See N.A.I., Census 1901, Cork 316/19c.

94 *C.E.*, 30 Oct. 1912.

95 Green, 'Second report', p. 22.

96 Lyons, *Ireland since the Famine*, pp 58–9.

97 *C.E.*, 14 Jan. 1890.

98 *R.I.I.F.*, 1889, p. 8.

99 *C.E.*, 14 Jan. 1890.

100 *R.C.I.P.W.*, p. 281.

101 *R.C.I.P.W.*, p. 223.

102 *R.C.I.P.W.*, p. 222.

103 *R.C.I.P.W.*, p. 10.

104 *I.R.C.*, *appendix to the second report, minutes of evidence*, [Cd.3896], H.C. 1908, xlvii, 331, p. 311.

105 Micks, *An account of the C.D.B.*, pp 55–6.

106 *R.C.I.P.W.*, p. 9.

107 *C.H.*, 2 Oct. 1890.

108 During the twelve week period between the 10 Jan. 1891 and 28 March 1891 the maximum number of men employed averaged 385 men per week. See *Fifty–ninth annual report from the commissioners of public works in Ireland* [C.6480], H.C. 1891, xxv, 587, p. 33.

109 *C.E.*, 6 Aug. 1890.

110 Ibid.

111 N.A.I., O.P.W., 1014/97.

112 Edward Fry, *James Hack Tuke, a memoir* (London, 1899), p. 268.

113 *Eagle*, 24 Dec. 1892.

114 *Eagle*, 21 Jan. 1893.

115 *Eagle*, 15 Oct. 1892.

116 *Eagle*, 15 Oct. 1892.

117 *Eagle*, 6 May 1893.

118 *Eagle*, 6 May 1893.

119 *Eagle*, 6 May 1893.

120 *R.I.I.F.*, *1893* [C.7404], H.C. 1894, xxii, 265, p. 58.

121 *F.J.*, 30 May 1893; *Eagle*, 17 June 1893.

122 *Eagle*, 22 July 1893.

123 *R.I.I.F.*, *1893*, p. 120.

124 *R.I.I.F.*, *1893*, p. 120.

125 *R.I.I.F.*, *1894*, H.C. 1895 [C.7793], xx, 269, pp 87 and 269.

126 Extracted from *R.I.I.F.* for each year from 1893 to 1907.

127 *C.E.*, 14 Jan. 1890.

128 *R.I.I.F.*, *1907* [Cd.4298], H.C. 1908], xiv, 1, pp 190–1.

129 H.C. Casserly, *Outline of Irish railway history* (London, 1974), p. 48.

130 N.A.I., B.T., black, file 9308.3.

131 C.D.B., *Report by Hon. R.C. Parsons respecting Baltimore pier accommodation, 1904*, p. 3.

132 Colm Creedon, *The Cork, Bandon and south coast railway: an illustrated history, vol. 11, 1900–1950* (Cork, 1989), p. 40

THE SOCIAL AND POLITICAL
IMPACT OF THE BALTIMORE
MACKEREL INDUSTRY

1   This figure includes 160 people (8 staff and 150 boys) resident in the Baltimore Fishery School.
2   *Census of Ireland, 1891, pt. I . . . county and city of Cork*, [C.3148–11], H.C. 1882, lxxvii,119, p. 268.
3   O'Flanagan, 'Urban life in county Cork', p. 435.
4   Land Commission, Estate of John Baron Carbery, E.C. 6560.
5   O'Flanagan, 'Urban life in county Cork', p. 437.
6   *R.I.I.F, 1887*, p. 6.
7   *Eagle*, 15 Aug. 1893.
8   *Eagle*, 4 Feb. 1888.
9   *Eagle*, 4 Feb. 1888.
10 *Eagle*, 4 Feb. 1888.
11 An editorial in the *Eagle* 5 Sept. 1898 which stated: 'It will keep its eye on the Emperor of Russia and all such despotic enemies . . . ' attracted international attention. See *The Southern Star centenary supplement 1889–1989*, pp 56–7.
12 *Census of Ireland, 1881, pt. I : . . . county and city of Cork* [C.3148–11], H.C. 1882, lxxvii,119, p. 241; *Census of Ireland, 1891, county and city of Cork*, p. 241.
13 *Census of Ireland, 1881, county of Cork*, p. 241; *Census of Ireland, 1891, county of Cork*, p. 241
14 *Eagle* 15 Nov. 1893.
15 Newman, *The harvest of the sea*, p. 3.
16 N.A.I., Census 1901, Cork 316/19c.
17 *C.E.*, 6 Aug. 1890.
18 *R.C.I*, p. 197.
19 *N.A.I.*, OPW 2627/91.
20 *R.C.I.P.W.*, p. 610.
21 *R.C.I.P.W.*, p. 610.

22 Newman, *The harvest of the sea*, p. 4.
23 *R.C.I.P.W.*, p. 612.
24 *R.C.I.P.W.*, p. 612; The pioneering role played by the Cape Clear fishermen is confirmed by Rev W. S. Green in his 'Preliminary report on the fishing industry in the south and south west of Ireland', pp 37–8.
25 Went, 'Pilchards in the south of Ireland', p. 143: *Eagle*, 28 July 1883; *C.E.*, 15 June 1885.
26 Went, 'Pilchards in the south of Ireland', p. 143; *R.I.I.F, 1879*, p. 6.
27 I.R.C., *appendix to second report*, p. 385; Francis Guy, *Francis Guy's directory of Munster* (Cork, 1886), pp 126–7.
28 D.E., Sp. Ed., File 9(b); D.E., Sp. Ed., File 9(a).
29 D.E., Sp. Ed., File 9(a).
30 D.E., Sp. Ed., File 9(a).
31 Chief inspector of reformatory and industrial schools of Ireland.
32 D.E., Sp. Ed., File 9(b).
33 The traditional subjects of the national schools' curriculum combined with subjects related to seamanship such as navigation and technical subjects including netmaking and carpentry. See *I.R.I.S., thirty third report 1894* [C.7805], H.C. 1895, lvii, 493, p. 18.
34 D.E., Sp. Ed., File 9(a); Similar tensions were reported in other communities with industrial schools; See Barnes, *Irish industrial schools 1868*, pp 137–8.
35 D.E., Sp. Ed., File 9(a).
36 *C.E.*, 6 Aug. 1890.
37 *C.E.*, 14 Jan. 1890.
38 *R.I.I.F.*, p. 13.
39 Dolly O'Reilly, *Sherkin Island* (Sherkin Island, 1994), p. 38.
40 *R.I.I.F, 1896* [C.8628], H.C. 1897, xviii, 299, p. 96.
41 This contrasts with an estimate of 'three or four hundred boats' afloat in Baltimore harbour during the fishing season in *I.B.*, 15 Oct. 1884.
42 *Eagle*, 8 July 1893.

43 Breatnach, *The man from Cape Clear*, p. 127; Ó Cróinín, *Seanachas ó Chairbre 1*, pp 212–6.
44 *Eagle*, 20 May 1893.
45 *Eagle*, 20 May 1893.
46 Francis Guy, *Guy's postal directory county Cork*, (Cork, 1895), p. 130.
47 See Green, 'Second report', pp 35–6.
48 *Proceedings of the Royal Dublin Society,1888*, p. 5.
49 I.F.C., vol. 52, p. 161.
50 Breatnach, *The man from Cape Clear*, p. 41.
51 N.A.I., Census 1901, Cork 316/19c.
52 Davis, *Deep sea fisheries*, p. 23.
53 Francis Guy, *Guy's Cork almanac and directory, 1920* (Cork, 1920), p. 246.
54 N.A.I., Census 1901, Cork 316/19c.
55 N.A.I., Census 1901, Cork 316/19c.
56 de Courcy Ireland, *Ireland's sea fisheries*, p. 71.
57 *I.B.*, 15 Oct 1884.
58 I.F.C., vol. 742, p. 459.
59 *The Baltimore and Skibbereen harbour order, 1884*, H.C. 1884 (259) iv, 435; Guy. *Francis Guy's directory of Munster*, p. 831.
60 *C.E.*, 12 April 1913.
61 Land Commission, Estate of John Baron Carbery, E.C. 6560.
62 *Report of her majesty's commissioners of inquiry into the working of the landlord and tenant (Ireland) act, 1870 and the acts amending the same* [C.2779], H.C. 1881, xix, 1, p. 901.
63 *Landlord and tenant (Ireland) act, 1870 inquiry*, p. 903.
64 *Landlord and tenant (Ireland) act, 1870 inquiry*, p. 905
65 *Eagle*, 13 Jan. 1883.
66 P.R.O., ADM 149/9.
67 P.R.O., ADM 149/9.
68 Built by Lord Carbery c.1879 to replace an older station located near the ruins of the O'Driscoll castle. *Eagle*, 17 March 1883.
69 P.R.O., ADM 149/9.
70 *R.C.I.P.W.*, p. 628.

71 Inscribed on a mural tablet commemorating his death on 13 Oct. 1992. See S.S., 8 Sept. 1894.
72 *R.C.I.P.W.*, p. 287; It was equally true that the payment of rent to the landlord was frequently dependent on the success of the season's fishing as in the case of the Cape Clear islanders; See Barnard, 'Fishing in seventeenth century Kerry', p. 25.
73 Breatnach, *The man from Cape Clear*, p. 13.
74 *R.C.I.P.W.*, p. 286.
75 D.E., Sp. File 9(a).
76 D.E., Sp. File 9(b).
77 *C.E.*, 29 April 1890.
78 *C.E.*, 6 Aug. 1890.
79 Micks, *An account of the C.D.B.*, p. 41; Brian Harvey, 'Changing fortunes on the Aran islands in the 1890s' in *Irish Historical Studies*, xxvii, no. 107 (May 1991), p. 241.
80 *Eagle*, 15 Aug. 1893.
81 *Eagle*, 29 Sept. 1894.
82 Land Commission, Estate of John Baron Carbery, E.C. 6560.
83 Land Commission, Carbery Estate, E.C. 6560; Property in the excluded area would continue to provide rental income to the Carbery estate, e.g. The Fishery School eventually bought out the leasehold interests of Lord Carbery with a payment of £747 on 26 Oct. 1920; See O'Donovan, *The statues are rocking*, p. 12.
84 D.A.T.I., *Report of fish cured in Ireland*, p. 81.
85 *Eagle*, 15 Aug. 1893.
86 I.R.C., *Appendix to second report*, p. 385.
87 *R.I.I.F, 1881*, p. 5.

CONCLUSION

1 Davis, *Deep sea fisheries of Ireland*, p. 13.